D0434990

TWAYNE'S WORLD AUTHORS SERIES

A Survey of the World's Literature

Sylvia E. Bowman, Indiana University

GENERAL EDITOR

AUSTRALIA

Joseph Jones, University of Texas

EDITOR

Louis Becke

(*TWAS 9*)

TWAYNE'S WORLD AUTHORS SERIES (TWAS)

The purpose of TWAS is to survey the major writers —novelists, dramatists, historians, poets, philosophers, and critics—of the nations of the world. Among the national literatures covered are those of Australia, Canada, China, Eastern Europe, France, Germany, Greece, India, Italy, Japan, Latin America, New Zealand, Poland, Russia, Scandinavia, Spain, and the African nations, as well as Hebrew, Yiddish, and Latin Classical literatures. This survey is complemented by Twayne's United States Authors Series and English Authors Series.

The intent of each volume in these series is to present a critical-analytical study of the works of the writer; to include biographical and historical material that may be necessary for understanding, appreciation, and critical appraisal of the writer; and to present all material in clear, concise English—but not to vitiate the scholarly content of the work by doing so.

Louis Becke

By A. GROVE DAY
University of Hawaii

Twayne Publishers, Inc. :: New York

Library of Congress Catalog Card Number: 66-21743

MANUFACTURED IN THE UNITED STATES OF AMERICA

To

THE ERUDITE AND AFFABLE STAFFS OF
THE MITCHELL AND DIXSON LIBRARIES,
SYDNEY, AUSTRALIA,
THE FISHER LIBRARY OF SYDNEY UNIVERSITY,
AND THE AUSTRALIAN NATIONAL LIBRARY,
CANBERRA,
THIS BOOK IS DEDICATED BY A
GRATEFUL RESEARCHER

Preface

"Who do you think is the best writer about the Pacific islands?"

When James A. Michener and I published in 1957 a chapter on Louis Becke in our collaborative volume *Rascals in Paradise,* we opened it with a kind of quiz session by which we might be able to determine a stranger's qualifications as an Old Pacific Hand. We decided that knowledge of names of ships, islands, or missionaries was not crucial. We concluded that there is only one correct question, "Who is the best writer about the region?" and only one correct answer. Almost without fail, people who know the vast ocean will respond that their favorite author is Louis Becke. Those who do not know the Pacific thoroughly will not have heard of Becke. Not to know Becke is to argue oneself unoriented in Pacific literature.

Becke's career was a real-life odyssey more exciting than any novelette he later concocted. Unlike most authors of the world, he was not brought up in a library. Until his fortieth year, he had done almost everything except publish a book. Here is a partial list of the jobs this small, wiry Australian held during his prewriting days: supercargo, "blackbirder" or labor recruiter, right-hand man to "Bully" Hayes the terrible buccaneer (Becke had to stand trial for piracy before he was twenty years old), beachcomber, island trader, gun-runner, bank clerk, gold-miner, timber-getter, cattleman, shark-catcher, pearl-shell hunter, whaler, blacksmith, drover, and poultry farmer. His favorite sports were fishing and hunting—his skill as a crack shot several times saved his life. Writing to him was simply another job, and like the handy ex-sailor that he was, he turned to the task cheerfully and with a will, ready to do his best, come fair winds or foul. At the time he was encouraged to put down the tales he had been narrating to friends, he was in poverty, trying to support a wife and two children by grubbing brush in the Sydney suburb of Manly. He began to write from necessity, and succeeded so well that for the next fifteen years he was able to make a living by his untutored pen.

Despite his lack of a long writing apprenticeship, Becke was at once hailed as "the Rudyard Kipling of the Pacific" and compared with Robert Louis Stevenson and Melville, not always to Becke's loss. During his writing years he published thirty-five volumes, and died before he was sixty, sitting at his writing-desk with an unfinished manuscript before him.

During the interim he had reared two families and had lived far from his native Australia. The Earl of Pembroke had written an introduction to Becke's first collection of stories, and Becke had gone to London, where he was hailed as a comrade by the authors of New Grub Street and lionized by the clubmen and socialites of the Old Country. From London he collaborated on several books at long range with a Sydney friend. Thereafter he lived in Ireland and France, and journeyed to Jamaica, the United States, and Canada before returning to his beloved South Seas, to exhaust himself in his last years in trying to organize a scientific expedition to the islands. During his writing career he made a good income, but sold all his work outright, and there was no flow of book royalties to keep him from pain and poverty. Before he was sixty, he died so poor that a collection had to be taken up in order that his grave in Waverley Cemetery might be fittingly marked for posterity.

Becke knew the nineteenth-century Pacific better than any other writer of his time, and lived among the islands close to the brown men and women who inhabited them. His understanding of Polynesian, Melanesian, and Micronesian lore and psychology was unexcelled. Becke not only met and talked with the adventurers of the Pacific during those wild times—whalers, schooner skippers, traders on lonely atolls, copra buyers, blackbirders, castaways, and beachcombers—but Becke often played such roles himself. He knew also at first hand the missionaries of several sects and was outspoken in his praise or blame of their attempts at converting and civilizing the native peoples. Becke roamed from the Western Carolines to Valparaiso, from Honolulu to Auckland, and with an intense power of recollection and a condensed, almost blunt style of narration, could conjure up what it was really like to live in the Pacific Ocean region before the days of the luxury cruise and the jets to Tahiti. His characters are not "white shadows" but lifelike, solid people of many shades of skin, whom he knew and lived beside on many a far-flung island.

Now that Becke has been buried for fifty years and most of his books are unavailable, it seems fitting to present this pioneer volume on his life and work. Although the quality of Becke's work for the most part was sustained and unflagging through his writing years, the product of any one year might vary greatly. More than most writers, he requires selection, and when he is bad he is horrid. But even though all careful readers might not agree completely on "the best of Becke," they should agree that at his best no other writer born and brought up in the Pacific region has been better at preserving in literature the islands of the South Seas. At his best, who can excel him in telling these tales?

No standard biography exists and many legends have grown up (often fostered by Becke himself) that need to be controverted by documented and often more startling facts. For this reason, two chapters have been devoted to his adventures and achievements, especially as they influenced his literary activities.

Becke's versatility was great. He was as happy to write about grim love affairs of white men and brown women as he was to contribute to a Sunday School paper for boys. He wrote fiction of various lengths, from a few pages to a full novel. Many of his books intermingle short stories with reminiscences and sketches of Pacific life or advice on how to raise vegetables on an atoll or harpoon a whale. He collaborated with Walter J. Jeffery on three novels (including one about Captain Bligh, Fletcher Christian, and the *Bounty* mutiny), two biographical volumes, and a mixed bag of stories and sketches. Becke was able to write an appreciation of *Moby Dick* twenty years before any American critic discovered Melville. He wrote several novels that were strongly autobiographical, and his stories in which Bully Hayes, his favorite true-life character, appears would fill more than one volume. Although Becke's settings are almost always somewhere in the Pacific, the world's largest and most mutable ocean, or else on his native continent of Australia, he even wrote one book of mildly satirical sketches from the French province of Normandy.

Within the following chapters a rough chronology of publication will be aimed at, but it has seemed more useful to group his writings by type and setting rather than to seek a developmental progress or decline that in reality does not exist. Becke in a sense started at the top of his bent, and maintained his standards, with some exceptions, through a decade and a half. One result of this study has been to puncture the popular idea that only the first two or three of Louis Becke's books are worth reading, and that thereafter he was forced to boil the pot, to cast his net wider and be satisfied with smaller fish. Some of his most memorable tales were written in far Europe a generation after the little ex-trader, broke and on his beam-ends in Sydney, was first advised to sit down beside a wooden gin-crate and put on paper some of the amazing yarns he had related to J. F. Archibald, eccentric editor of the popular Sydney *Bulletin.*

It is true, however, that Becke was primarily the master of the short story with a Pacific setting, and Chapter Three therefore deals critically with these yarns wherever found scattered through eighteen books. The next chapter covers the collaboration on six volumes with Jeffery; the letters written by Becke to his friend during this period reveal a good deal about his London life and his self-taught craftsmanship on several works that should long be remembered, especially *The Mutineer,* the novel about Christian and the *Bounty.* Chapter Five concentrates on Becke's portrayals of his buccaneering skipper Captain William Henry Hayes, the "Bully" of legend and fact, about whom Becke always enjoyed writing, even though his best characterization of Hayes was published in a novel with another author's name on the title page. Chapter Six discusses types of writing in which Becke was admittedly not a great master—the novel and the novelette—and also covers his non-fiction sketches and his many writings dealing not with the Pacific islands but with his native Australia. Becke knew well the purlieus of New South Wales and the dangerous outback of Queensland, where a wandering prospector might be "bailed up" by a bushranger or speared in the back by a savage aboriginal. A final chapter attempts to review the ups and downs of Louis Becke's critical reputation, pointing out the reefs and shoals through which his reception has had to ride during the years, and the tides of appreciation that more and more have risen until today, when the fraternity of Becke enthusiasts around the globe get together to discuss the difficulties of finding a collector's copy of *His Native Wife* or to deplore the lack of available Becke reprints for the younger generation of readers to enjoy. This chapter also summarizes the main qualities of Becke's typical themes, characterizations, plots, settings, and style.

One minor but exacting task set by the present writer has been to compile as complete and accurate a working bibliography of all the writings by and about Becke that are available after search in many libraries from Honolulu and London to Wellington, Sydney, Melbourne, and Canberra.

Reading and rereading over the past twenty years the thirty-five books of Becke, all long out of print, has been a pleasant literary voyage; and the plunder I have brought back I am happy to share with a generation of readers who are coming to realize that the Pacific is the ocean of the future, the highway between the Americas and Asia and Australasia. As Professor Garrett Mattingly of Columbia University has said: "American history is history in transition from an Atlantic to a Pacific phase." We as Americans cannot know too much about the Pacific region of today and yesterday.

A. GROVE DAY

University of Hawaii

Acknowledgments

Grateful acknowledgment is made to the Mitchell and Dixson Libraries of Sydney, Australia, and to the Australian National Library of Canberra, Australia, for permission to reprint original material as indicated in the Bibliography. The Sir Alexander Turnbull Library in Wellington, New Zealand, kindly furnished microfilm of some Louis Becke manuscripts. Dr. George Mackaness of Sydney generously offered me the use of microfilm of a collection of letters written by Becke to his family from Jamaica and Canada in 1902.

The following persons freely contributed information on Becke: Baden Backus of Mittagong, N.S.W.; Miss Janet Bell of the Hawaiian and Pacific Room, Gregg M. Sinclair Library, University of Hawaii; Alec H. Chisholm of the Royal Australian Historical Society, Sydney; Miss Agnes C. Conrad, head, Archives of Hawaii; J. W. Earnshaw of Lindfield, N.S.W.; Harry E. Maude, Department of Pacific History, Australian National University; Lew Priday, formerly of Sydney; Walter W. Stone, Sydney; and Dr. Carl Stroven, Librarian, University of Hawaii. I am deeply indebted for information and assistance from Louis Becke's daughters, Mrs. Alrema Hardie and Miss Niya Becke, of Springwood, N.S.W.

Acknowledgment is also gratefully made to the Research Committee of the University of Hawaii and the Department of English for recommending the allowance of time to carry on research on the present volume.

Contents

Chronology

1855 June 18, born in Port Macquarie, N.S.W.

1867 Family moved to Sydney; attended Fort Street School.

1869 Left on July 23rd with brother Vernon on *Lizzie and Rosa* from Newcastle, N.S.W.; arrived San Francisco, October 20.

1871 Returned to Sydney July 24 on *City of Melbourne*, "G. L. Becke, clerk, of San Francisco."

1872 Stowed away March 21 on bark *Rotumah* for Samoa, where he worked in store in Apia and may have traded in cutter between Apia and Savaii.

1873 Departed Apia on December 3 with orders from Mrs. Mary Macfarlane to deliver ketch *E.A. Williams* to Captain W. H. Hayes at Mili Atoll in Marshall Group.

1874 Delivered ketch January 17 and signed on as supercargo to Captain Hayes in *Leonora.*

1874 *Leonora* sunk in hurricane off Kusaie, March 15; before end of year Becke was returned to Brisbane to stand trial for piracy, but was acquitted

1875–1880 Various jobs in Australia and in Pacific Islands; landed on Nanumanga, Ellice Islands, April 11, 1880, as trader for De Wolf Company.

1881 Moved to Nukufetau, married Nelea Tikena of that island; on August 24, *Orwell* wrecked on Beru Island in Kingsmill Group, from which Becke departed October 6 on *George Noble.*

1882 February 16, at side of dying Captain Gustave Rabardy of *Génil* off New Britain; November 1, wrote mother from Majuro in Marshall Islands.

1886 February 10, married Mary Elizabeth Maunsell in Port Macquarie.

1888 November 9, birth of daughter Nora Lois.

1892 October 1, wrote to ask for a trading station in New Hebrides.

1893 May 6, first story, "'Tis In the Blood," appeared in Sydney *Bulletin,* soon followed by others. October 3, letter from T. A. Browne offered to pay for material later used in *A Modern Buccaneer* by "Rolf Boldrewood." December 14, T. Fisher Unwin wrote from London offering to publish a volume of Becke's stories.

1894 August 6, Becke wrote to Browne to protest use of material in *A Modern Buccaneer*. November, publication in London of Becke's first book, *By Reef and Palm* (for subsequent publications, see Bibliography).

1895–1896 October to April, Becke with Nora at Port Macquarie, at work on various publications, including collaborations with Walter James Jeffery.

1896 Left Sydney June 9 with Nora and Miss Fanny Sabina Long *via* Melbourne, Adelaide, and Gibraltar to London, arriving in mid-August. After some months in London, lived at Deal, Richmond, and Eastbourne.

1897 October 30, daughter Alrema born at Eastbourne.

1898 September 27, daughter Niya born at Eastbourne.

1901–1903 Residence at Greenore, County Louth, Ireland. In Jamaica, B.W.I., August 1 through September 30, 1902, arriving on *Port Royal* and departing on *Admiral Sampson* for Boston. To Montreal, then departing October 9 on *Lake Champlain* for Liverpool.

1903 October 29, Sydney court found in favor of Mary Elizabeth Becke, petitioner for divorce on grounds of desertion.

1903–1906 Residence with family in various parts of northern France.

1908 With family, returned to South Seas for scientific studies; in New Zealand in September, arrived at Suva, Fiji, September 28 on *Navau.*

1910 September 7, elected member of Royal Society of New South Wales.

1913 February 18, died in Hotel York, Sydney; buried next day in Waverley Cemetery. Last book, *Bully Hayes: Buccaneer,* published posthumously.

CHAPTER 1

Adventures in the South Seas

THE writer who best knew the South Pacific in the nineteenth century was Louis Becke. Unlike Herman Melville, he did not spend a few years drifting through the region and return to another homeland to write about his exotic travels. Born in Australia in 1855, Becke earned his living in the South Seas, and had spent twenty years residing in its islands before the date when Robert Louis Stevenson decided to make Samoa his last home.

Becke did not visit the Pacific in order to write about it. He would probably never have become a writer, however, had he not earlier become a sea wanderer and a Pacific trader. He roved "from Easter Island to the Pelews" and voyaged as a crewman in more than one blackbirding schooner, aside from his famous cruise as supercargo with the American buccaneer "Bully" Hayes.

For forty years, Becke pursued life with zest, without a thought of writing as a career. It was only when he was on his uppers in Sydney, with a family to support, that he embraced what Joseph Conrad, his contemporary and rival among readers of seagoing stories, called the "dog's life" of a professional literary man.

I *Memories of "The System"*

During the following fifteen years, Becke, who soon left for Europe, produced thirty-five books (six of them in collaboration), together with a mass of reviews, news notes, and miscellaneous articles. All except *Sketches from Normandy* (1906) dealt with the vast Pacific region. He was found dead in Sydney at the age of fifty-eight, with an unfinished story manuscript on his writing desk in front of him. Becke died with his literary boots on. But his books did not die, and for a long while will remain the favorites of a passionate group of readers who believe, along with James A. Michener, that "if one wants an honest, evocative, unpretentious and at times fearfully moving account of the Pacific in its heyday, he must read Louis Becke." [1]

The works of few men have been more dependent upon their own lives than those of Becke. Therefore it is especially important to know about the events of this author's career. The sad fact that he often garbled or even prevaricated about those events makes the quest of the biographer more challenging, and the lack of numerous documents during much of his early, island-drifting career must be compensated by dependence on his reminiscences, interviews, and other testimonies.[2] Many letters, press notices, and papers fortunately still survive, however, and it is now possible to put together for the first time a fairly lengthy and authentic story of the life of Louis Becke, particularly as it relates to his literary achievement. It is a true story more exciting than many of his fictions.

George Lewis Becke, as he was christened, was born on June 18, 1855, as attested by the records of the Registrar-General of New South Wales. This date is also given on his Church of England baptismal certificate issued by the Parish of St. Thomas on July 14, 1855. During interviews, Becke gave at least two other birth dates, probably to imply that he had left home even earlier than he actually did.

His parents were Frederick and Caroline Matilda Becke, both English. His mother came from Devonshire, home county of so many British voyagers. She was the daughter of Charles Beilby, well-known Sydney merchant in the 1830's. Her father, Becke claimed, had been secretary to the Duke of Cumberland and had sailed his family out to the colonies in his own vessel. Elsewhere he wrote: "My grandfather had invested a large sum of money in founding cattle stations in that part of the colony [Port Macquarie], and in persistently searching for copper and tin. He, like many others of the early settlers, lost nearly all his fortune and returned to Sydney in disgust." [3] At the time of the birth of Louis—as he always preferred to be called—Frederick Becke was clerk of petty sessions in the little penal settlement of Port Macquarie, at the mouth of the Hastings River about two hundred miles north of Sydney.

"My earliest recollections," Becke wrote a year before his death, "go back to the time when I was six years of age, and the pilot allowed me to scramble into the pilot boat when she was launched down the greasy skids to board one of the old-time steamers; and I shall always remember the ecstasy of the boat facing the heavy surf that rolled into Pilot Cove—a place hewn out of the solid rock by convict hands in the old days when the swish of the lash and the rattle of the gyves reigned in the land." [4]

Louis was the youngest of six children. His father, a stern, black-bearded paterfamilias, strongly felt that his boys should know all the crafts of boat and bush, and urged them to spend much time outdoors. This Louis preferred to the schoolroom or Sunday school, and his lifelong stammer he traced to the terror inspired by a brutal teacher. Before he was ten he twice ran away from home (once in the company of a little red-haired girl) and had to be brought back by mounted troopers of the police service in which his father was an official. His mother and sisters were kindly, but the boy preferred to go off to the coastal lagoons and watch his aboriginal friends spear five-foot fish for their dinners.

The old Becke house at Clifton stood overlooking the sea on the summit of a great, grassy bluff, which seemed to spring from out the gray monotony of the Australian bush. It had been built by convicts about 1827 as a residence for the military governor of the settlement and his family. In the three miles between the house and the town lay only a lighthouse and the ruins of many stone cottages, relics of forced construction work. The settlement still contained convicts "of the better class," as well as emancipated men who worked in the neighborhood. The abhorrence of Louis and his otherwise sweet-tempered mother for the hell-fire preacher was recalled long afterwards. "Often did I, when sitting on our great square pew in that dreadful, horrible church, press close to my mother's side and bury my face in her dress, as he lashed himself into a fury and called down the vengeance of a wrathful God upon the rows of silent, wretched beings clad in yellow, who were seated on long stools in the back of the church, guarded by soldiers, who, with loaded muskets, were stationed in the gallery above." [5]

The provincial life of the town, which he nicknamed "Lots o' Time," bored the boy. "I have often thought," he wrote later, "that that town only wanted a small cathedral to make it, *facile princeps,* the dullest and most God-forsaken hole in the whole Australian continent. It was built by convict hands in the days of the cruel System, and nothing but an earthquake or a big fire will ever improve it." [6] He was destined, however, to return to his old haunts to find a bride.

One tutor named Guy was a hero to the children, for he had been a junior Marine officer who had stormed a native *pa* and been captured in the First Maori War. With Guy and a small crew, according to his circumstantial account, Louis sailed before the age of ten as cabin boy on the family's sixty-ton ketch to Lord Howe Island, returning with a valuable cargo of onions. At other times the boys would drive home a bullock for beef and, under the observant paternal eye, would hoist the carcase, skin and clean it, and then peg out the hide and cover it with wood ashes. On rare holidays, the boys would kill and skin snakes, or else scour the reef for haliotis shells and sometimes find a few small pearls to bring in a bit of spending money.[7]

The Becke family moved to Sydney around 1867, and found a house on Hunter's Hill on a point jutting into the Parramatta River just opposite Cockatoo Island, which then held prison buildings perched high on its treeless sides. He remembered "the ever-pacing, red-coated sentries, the sonorous clang of the prison bell, and the long lines of wretched convicts marching to and from their toil in the drydock or among the sandstone quarries." Louis and some of his brothers were taken over to converse with the "better-conditioned men" who inhabited the cells hewn out of solid rock. On foggy nights, when sentries were doubled, the boys could hear the guard boats rowing round and round, and "would go down to the rocks to listen for a shot from a sentry's rifle, followed by the muffled clamor of that dreadful bell and the sound of someone near us panting hard in his swim for liberty. We had once heard these sounds and seen, early in the dawn of a winter's day, a wretched, exhausted creature clinging with bleeding hands to the oyster-covered rocks beneath our house, too weak to drag himself further from his pursuers." [8] Becke's disdain for prisons and other authority in later years might perhaps be traced to his early sympathy with such victims of the "System."

II *Louis Becke, the Boy Pirate*

The boy was short but wiry, and his big hands enabled him to defend himself with spirit in any scrap. He attended the Fort Street Model School, as it was then called, on Observatory Hill in Sydney. There he obtained the brief but sound education that was to last him for the rest of his life and to give him a supercargo's post on many a South Sea schooner. But he dreamed not of a literary career; he dreamed of becoming a pirate.

Becke had a good memory, but as with his contemporary Mark Twain, many of the things he remembered best were "the things that never happened." Louis's accounts of adventures in his teens drawn from various interviews and reminiscences, and from the introduction to his first book, are so extravagant that the years are not long enough to accommodate all his biographical inventions.

The Becke legend includes the following adventures before he was nineteen. When he was only twelve he and his brother Vernon embarked on the Pacific to seek their fortunes. They left Newcastle, N.S.W. on the bark *Lizzie and Rosa*, commanded by a little red-headed Irishman, a savage bully who boasted of being a Fenian and who was hated by the thirty passengers. From the day they sailed, the crew had to man the pumps, but the captain refused to turn back. The leaky old ship met such a series of adverse gales that it was forty-one days before they sighted the island of Rurutu in the Tubuai group, where young Becke got his first glimpse of a South Sea island.

All the ship's company demanded that the captain supply them with fresh food offered by the natives, but he was so stingy that he refused, whereupon the mate, a hot-tempered Yorkshireman, exploded and knocked him down. The monkeylike captain rushed below and reappeared with a brace of old-fashioned Colt revolvers, one of which he pointed at the mate. Calling upon him to surrender and be put in irons, he fired toward the mate's head. The bullet missed. The crew rushed the skipper, seized him, and held him under the force pump until he was nearly drowned. Only their respect for the pleas of the captain's wife kept the crew from killing the man.

Louis and Vernon had been eager spectators of the mutiny but thereafter became so bored that they decided to desert the ship, and had to be locked in their cabins in the port. With the captain confined in a stateroom, the crew worked the ship to Honolulu in twenty days, under the orders of the mate from Yorkshire. There he and all the crew stood trial for mutiny, but were acquitted by the court, mainly through the testimony of the passengers.

Finally the old crate reached California, after a passage of 140 days. Here in San Francisco, while Vernon found a job on a ranch, Louis became captain's clerk on a steamer running to Lower California. Using his savings to buy a share in a trading ship, he then cruised the Marshall Islands for several years. His partner was an old man who could not navigate and during bouts of delirium tremens had to be wrapped in a strait jacket to keep him from jumping overboard. On the way to the Palau Group, the schooner rescued a canoe load of Marshallese who had been blown hundreds of miles off their course. In Polynesian style, Becke swapped names with the chief, who had lost thirty of his crew of seventy, and gave them provisions enough to get home. Many years later, when Becke was near death on the island of Majuro, he was nursed back to health by this same chief.

Becke then returned to Australia and joined the gold rush in Queensland, drifting about and learning, among other things, how to be a locomotive driver, a miner, and a blacksmith. Still feeling the lure of the sea, he bought a trading cutter and set up as a smuggler of arms and ammunition during the "Steinberger period" of the civil war in Samoa. Here he encountered Bully Hayes and later signed on as his supercargo.

Much of this saga is invention, or else a concentration of many years of adventure into the years of youth. Those years would not have allowed time for voyages to Lower California and the Carolines. The light of research reveals that only four years and five months elapsed between the time Louis left home and his departure from Samoa to join Bully Hayes on an atoll in the Marshalls to start the most exciting cruise of his life.

The *Lizzie and Rosa* left Newcastle on July 23, 1869, when Louis was actually fourteen. Careful search in the Archives of Hawaii and in newspapers of the period gives no evidence that this ship put into Honolulu in the summer of 1869 or that a mutiny trial of the entire crew was held there. However, the San Francisco *Bulletin* for October 20, 1869, does record the arrival of the *Lizzie and Rosa* from New South Wales via Tahiti, requiring only eighty-four days for an uneventful trip. Only six names are recorded on the passenger list, and "Becke" is not among them; however, since he traveled by steerage, it is possible that only first-class passengers were named. He certainly reached San Francisco, for the 1871 street directory lists "George Becke, messenger." But he soon returned home, for records in Sydney show that "G. L. Becke, clerk, of San Francisco," arrived as a second-class passenger on the *City of Melbourne* on July 24, 1871, from San Francisco via Fiji. He thus reached home at the age of sixteen.

It is probably true, as Becke said later, that he got acquainted with a Rarotongan native who was an A.B. on the bark *Rotumah* and who on March 21, 1872, helped him to stow away on that ship, bound for Samoa. There he worked for about two years as a clerk in the store of Macfarlane and Williams, and perhaps did some smuggling on the side (such a story as "By Order of the King" in *Notes from My South Sea Log* has an authentic ring). He claims that for six months he was a partner and comrade of a Manihiki half-caste named Alan or Allen Strickland in 1873.[9] He wrote in *Breachley, Black Sheep,* of battlelines around Apia, and in an unpublished piece written in 1911 said: "Fighting sometimes took place in the town of Apia itself, and it was no unusual sight to see a number of decapitated heads being carried through the street."[10] And at Apia he met Hayes, blackbirder, buccaneer, and notorious bully of the South Seas.

Becke wrote a great deal through the years concerning Bully Hayes, and a chapter will later be devoted to his treatments of this hero. It will suffice here to say that as a result of his acquaintance, the boy who dreamed in Sydney of becoming a pirate was brought in Her Majesty's man-of-war *Rosario* to Brisbane under arrest, "charged with being an accomplice of Bully Hayes in various piracies in the Pacific."[11]

III *The Pig That Can Climb Trees*

Fortunately, Becke had kept a copy of a power-of-attorney given him by the owner of the ship he had delivered to Hayes, and for lack of evidence he was acquitted of piracy at the ripe age of nineteen.

From 1875 to 1880 there is little solid information about Becke's career. He probably spent two years on the Palmer River gold fields, a period at Charters Towers, and a few months as a clerk in a Townsville bank. According to an interview many years later, "When the manager of a bank in North Queensland, in which Mr. Becke had been employed for six weeks, complained that his assistant was frequently absent from his counter; that he had left £900 in the hands of an hotel keeper in order to see a fight; that he had had 'words' with an accountant and was generally intractable; that he wore unconventional dress and kept kangaroo-dogs on the premises; and that he showed utter lack of business capacity and distinct disinclination for work, Mr. Becke cheerfully admitted each count of the indictment and asked to be permitted to resign and resume his freedom." [12]

The call of his beloved islands was still strong, and it is likely that he returned to them several years before setting up as a proprietor of a trading station in 1880. His "Autobiography" says merely: "Went back again to Eastern Polynesia, Gambiers, Paumotus, Easter and Pitcairn Island, picked up an abandoned French barque on a reef, floated her, loaded her with coconuts and attempted to sail her with a native crew to N. Zealand. Went ashore in a hurricane and lost everything." His stories and sketches show again and again an intimate knowledge of the work of whalers and shark-hunters, of supercargoes and pearlers, of lonely copra traders, and of recruiters on vessels hunting native labor in cannibal waters. He was also acquainted with such romantic rovers of the vast Pacific as Paunchy Bill, Joachim Ganga, Paddy Coney, and Joe Bird. He also knew "Cappy" O'Keefe, who had carved out a little kingdom for himself in the Carolines, who flooded Yap with cheaply quarried stone money, and who finally disappeared in his tiny schooner *Santa Cruz.* But Becke also claimed to have guided the field work of such naturalists as Friedrich Finsch and Jan Kubary.

Becke was landed on the island of Nanumanga in the Ellice Group on April 11, 1880, in the employ of Tom de Wolf, partner in a Liverpool trading firm and a person often mentioned in his stories. Here he was taken in by an acquaintance, the Samoan missionary Ioane. Life for the single white occupant of a lost atoll in the Pacific could be misery or joy. In a revealing essay, "The Loneliness of It" (*'Neath Austral Skies*), Becke later quoted from a letter by a young Scotsman who was sickened by the monotony of a trader's existence and the lack of anything to do. Louis Becke's zest and curiosity did not leave him for a moment. He would explore the entire island, help Ioane build a church, learn to make sennit, build a canoe, and sail to the great submerged reef of Tia Kau, to increase his skill in fishing the depths haunted by the shadows of the murderous sharks. To Louis, the natives were not the "surly, cantankerous" brutes of his Scots correspondent, not "servile, sponging and hypocritical," but kindhearted, honest, companionable, and resourceful in a changing environment. Becke was friendly, intelligent, full of eagerness to learn new things, and endowed with a memory that later would enable him to draw upon his experiences in a way denied to a man merely seeking quick wealth in the copra trade.

Life on the Ellice Islands in the 1880's is pictured in Becke's surviving letters to his mother, which reveal by their graphic if unpunctuated style the power of the writer he was later to become. They are chatty records of his trading activities and his daily routine, enlivened by accounts of hurricane and shipwreck. Receiving a letter from his family was always an event, for some would take eighteen months to reach his trading shack. The ship that finally took him away from Nukufetau brought two from his mother, one of which he joyfully replied "*was only a month old.*" Since these letters have never been published, they will here be drawn upon freely, for they give a first-hand view of the South Sea author's early years as no other documents could do.[13]

From the schooner *Venus* off Nanumanga he writes on April 11, 1880. He plans to stay eighteen months on a small island with about two hundred natives and no white man. "The King and chiefs have made a law that only one white man is to live on the island and that has decided me to remain as I think I will do very well here. The people are very friendly and I hope in 6 months more to be able to speak their language well. . . . I have about $3,000 of trade [goods] and I am busy getting it on shore. It is now Sunday and the *Venus* leaves on Tuesday. We cannot land anything, today being Sunday, as the natives are great missionaries in their way. . . ."

From Nanumanga he writes on the following July 8 that he is thinking of leaving. "I have had a serious dispute with the natives or rather with a chief here and his people and I have closed my trade houses and do not now buy any copra and unless they pay me ten thousand cocoanuts I will leave the island with my trade, as to remain would be a great loss to De Wolf and Sons. I have built a very large house and outhouses and am or rather was quite settled down till this affair happened—most fortunately I kept calm although a few more words would have brought on a terrible mess—and I don't want to be taken to Fiji in a man-of-war to make the acquaintance of the estimable Chief Justice Corr, the High Commissioner for Polynesia, for in all disputes now with natives especially if there is any blood shed an *Englishman* is run up with a rope with little compunction—a man in the South Seas now might as well be a Chinaman as an Englishman for all the protection he will receive—the first chance I get I will naturalise myself as a citizen of the United States. Almost all the people on this island like me and are well disposed and friendly to me but I want to go further to the northward where the people are free from that curse of the islands the missionary element; the missionaries have been here about five years and they have as usual succeeded in rendering the natives less ferocious but ten thousand times more cunning, lying, avaricious, and hypocritical than they were in their natural state. . . .

"I am living pretty lonely at present as I have dismissed all my workpeople and servants and have kept only a little native girl Pautoe who keeps house for me and cooks for me native fashion and whom I have adopted. . . . I rise every day at 4 a.m. and bathe and then Pautoe gets my breakfast, generally flying fish or lobsters, and fills my pipe (I smoke a pipe now) and cleans the house while I smoke and instruct her how to use a broom and wash plates etc. without breaking more than two at one washup; about 10 o'clock some 20 or 30 native girls come and sit on the verandah in the shade and plait straw or sinnet and try and wheedle a cigarette out of the white man and as they consider it a great privilege to come and talk to the white man I make them pay for it by bringing me fish, puraka and young cocoanuts to drink. I think I drink about 30 cocoanuts every day—every evening the missionary and his wife Eline send me ten cocoanuts and something for tea and I return the compliment by either a little beef or biscuit or whatever I may have ready at the time. . . . I have a nice little cat given me by the Carpenter of the *Venus* and she is a famous rat-catcher. The natives call her '*the pig with toe nails that can climb trees*' and she is much admired and caressed by the native children. Her name is 'Dodger.' "

IV *"No Better Than the Natives"*

Becke reports to his mother on business affairs and states that after his appeal before a native chief an opponent admitted that he should pay a heavy fine in coconuts. "If I was an American or a German I could make the natives pay me about $2,500 in copra but as I am an Englishman I cannot."

However, unlike most of the South Sea traders, Becke was able to enjoy other rewards than monetary, and to recall afterward more than his trade-room ledger accounts. In this he may be contrasted with the haunting figure of Captain Handy in James Norman Hall's classic story, "Occupation: Journalist." [14] In this yarn, Hall's would-be collaborator says: "Know him! I've got the best of Louis Becke many a time, trading through these islands. He was a trader, you know. But I wouldn't have thought he had it in him to be an author." When Hall replies that Becke's stories "have the stamp of truth on them," old Captain Handy snorts contemptuously: "I can tell you more truth about the South Seas in ten minutes than Louis Becke could tell you in twenty years." But after reading Handy's sobersided manuscript, Hall concludes that it is incredible that a man who had spent half a century in the Pacific should have found nothing more worthy of record than mere trading sums.

Becke was not only truthful but was aware of his surroundings. He did not miss any atoll adventure that was going. A few weeks later, on August 23, he continued his account to his mother with a description of a dangerous canoe voyage to the island of Nanumea, on which the inhabitants were supposed to have built huge fires to guide the navigators. "We sailed all day till dark when one of our canoes capsized; we then took down sails and waited for the fire as we did not see any land and were afraid to run past it in the dark. We saw the Nanumanga fires every hour but none from where we thought Nanumea to be; at ten o'clock a heavy squall set in with a wild sea and cold rain, two men constantly bailing to keep us from foundering; poor Eline was wet through till Ioane and I made a covering of the sail and I gave her a change of my clothes; the natives now commenced to get frightened and wanted to turn back but Ioane and Eline and I held out; at midnight it cleared up and then Eline called me to look and we saw a glorious blaze from Nanumea about 20 miles away —we set sail and passed over the reef at 4 a.m. Here to my astonishment I found two white men traders, Alfred and a man named Harry Johnson, a very decent young fellow who took me to his house; he is married to a native girl and is doing very well. We intended only to remain 4 days at Nanumea but our people quarreled with the Nanumeans, who seized our canoes, and trouble was brewing but after 16 days delay we got away again and after a bad passage back we reached our own island in safety. I forgot to say though that only two canoes came back, one small one and mine, the other three were too frightened. I brought back three cats with me which I got from Pepa, Harry's wife."

The same letter records that Becke had agreed to open his trade again and was getting ready to go to the Grand Coral Reef to catch sharks when two children came running to say that they had sighted a ship, the *Venus*. The house was swept and floored with new mats by the native girls by the time the captain and supercargo came ashore to check on Becke's storekeeping. "My copra greatly disappointed me only turning out 3300 lb. I expected there would be 6000. However Capt. Cummings was so pleased with me and my nice house that he said he would not fail to give a good account of me to A. T. DeW[olf]. . . . It may happen that De Wolf will close up his island business and so I am writing to him to ask him to let me stay on here and I will pay him for his trade in two years time and carry on the business myself." Becke hoped in that case to get his brother Alfred to come to Nanumanga to help in the business.

On August 26 another schooner came to pick up some copra belonging to a former trader. Becke bought a cash box from the captain, and to deliver the money for it had to swim out beyond the reef, where the vessel ran in to pick him up. "I can tell you I enjoyed a glass of grog when I got on board," is his sole comment on this strenuous effort to redeem a promise to pay in cash.

On August 28, Becke wrote again to his mother: "I forgot to tell you that I am a great pig man now, I have 22 pigs in my styes and two days ago a Mrs Pig increased my stock by twins. . . . To day being Sunday I am alone in the house, my Cook and housemaid have gone to church. . . . Last night I baked 4 loaves and left them in a box and while I was asleep a pig came in and eat three but very considerately left me one for Sunday (this is no doubt the result of missionary teaching). I think Olive would like to see my two cats and a pet pig I have, they always sleep together, piggy lies down and the cats sprawl across him like wet dish-clouts."

Becke during his twenty years among the islands encountered many fellow traders, of whom not all were representative of the higher side of European civilization. A sample is mentioned in this same letter. "I forgot to say that I had a visitor here in the *Vaitupulemele*, a trader from an adjacent island Niutao, Geo. Winchcombe—four years on Niutao and cannot yet talk the language; in fact I had to interpret for him. Such a man to talk, my ears are actually tingling now, I don't know how much more I would have suffered if it had not been for a case of gin I produced and by liquoring him up freely I got a little respite. He is a fair sample of too many island traders, fond of liquor and never happy without some grievance to relate against the natives; these are the men that give the missionaries such a pull over *all* traders. They are no better than the natives—they let their children run about wild and devote all their energies to the gin-bottle, but still at this present time the general island trader is as a rule a respectable and fairly educated man; there are a few left of the old class, the dissolute whaler or escaped convict."[10]

V *The Wreck of the* Orwell

An exciting account of the destruction of Becke's trading station by a hurricane was given his mother on February 21, 1881. The storm, on the second of that month, was according to the natives the worst in thirty-five years. At three in the morning, it was raining and blowing furiously. At low water the sea receded. "Anticipating something serious we ran into the big house and the next minutes with a strange roaring sound the sea rose up like a wall and dashed over the reef in one mighty wave and swept up into the village, sweeping away fifteen houses like chaff—the next wave dashed into my front room and filled it with coral rocks and sand. How glad I am to say that by working like demons we saved all the trade, got everything carried into the rear of the village and out of danger; the wind was at its heighth and the sound it made was like the droning of countless flocks of bees, and sea after sea rolled up into the village; in a few minutes my house, trade house, copra house, fowl houses, pig houses etc. were things that had been, and piled up without much regard to regularity in a heap, together with sundry drowned pigs and other live stock; the next wave they all went away to sea together with a few native houses. I lost some copra but saved 7000 lbs and also saved my canoe which is a valuable one, so altogether I won't grumble, as I might have lost all. . . . It is now the 21st and you will perhaps be surprised to know that I am back again in the old position with new house, copra houses, cook houses, and man servants and maid servants and all things that are his. Some hundreds of thousands of young cocoanuts have been destroyed and I am anxiously awaiting the arrival of one of our vessels to consult as to what is to be done. My vessel is now some five months overdue."

The delay in arrival of the De Wolf schooner resulted from a collapse of the firm, which pulled out of the trade at a considerable loss. Becke moved to the neighboring island of Nukufetau and went into business for himself. He also married for the first time, to a girl of that island named Nelea Tikena.[16] Nothing but this bare fact is known of the marriage, but the future author of *His Native Wife* knew whereof he was to write.

A letter from the island of Beru (or Peru, as Becke spells it) in the Kingsmill Group gives his immediate impressions of a shipwreck which he was later to write about in several places, changing names and facts to fit his readership. In "'Frank' the Trader" he was to write that after spending almost a year on "Nukutipipi, an atoll in the Carolines" (actually Nukutipipi is in the Paumotus and he had been in the Ellice Group), he was evicted by a German barque that claimed that only a German had a right to trade on that island. He pulled up stakes and was ready to go anywhere, "as long as it was some place where there were mountains and forests and rivers, and where I should again hear the shrill cry of the wild mountain cock and the booming note of the great purple pigeon; for I was deadly sick of the low-lying sandy atolls of the Ellice, Gilbert, and Marshall Islands, and their fish and coconut-eating inhabitants. I had had three years of it, and the monotony of my daily life was beginning to tell upon my nerves." [17] But, he continues in the sketch, the ship he embarked upon, the *Orchid,* which he nicknamed the *Torpid,* a slow vessel under an ignorant captain, was wrecked on the reef at Beru. He saved all his personal effects, clothes, guns and ammunition, and a cat that was an old comrade. But his trade goods in the holds were lost, and all he had left in the world was six hundred Chile dollars.

The ship was really named *Orwell,* and a letter to Becke's mother of September 24, 1881, gives a perhaps more factual record of this adventure. "At last on August 6 the long expected vessel came for me from Auckland, the *Orwell,* and the supercargo Flower had instructions to take me to Apiang in this group and I was to form a head station there and to be manager for the firm [Henderson and Macfarlane of Auckland] of all their business in the Kingsmill and Marshall Groups. I packed up and we sailed next day and after touching at various islands we made this island on August 24 and at 11 p.m. at night we lost the vessel and with difficulty saved our lives. . . . The natives plundered and pillaged the vessel, we were without arms and I had the maddening sensation of seeing myself robbed and dared not raise my hand else we would have all lost our lives. The firm (H & M) have an agency here and we all went to live in the trader's house, a very nice fellow, a Tyrolese named Francisco Vollerio.

"We set to work to save some provisions, but the natives robbed us almost as fast as we got it; however we saved some. At this time all my worldly goods was a piece of red silk I had wrapped round my loins, afterwards though I got a good many thin clothes, but fortunately the climate here is such that I never go beyond wearing a pair of cotton trousers. The day after the wreck the captain called us together and asked for volunteers to go in one of the boats saved from the wreck to the island of Apemama distant 300 miles. The crew refused; the mate and I and two others volunteered but as luck would have it next day a barque called the *George Noble* belonging to a Chinese firm in Sydney came here and Captain Evers took Captain Robinson, five men and a boat on board and was to take them as near to Apemama as he could and then they were to pull."

Becke continued with information about how to write him in

future, and said that he had lost a twenty-page letter written to his mother about some "very extraordinary adventures" on Nukufetau. "I had also letters prepared for Edwin, Alfred, and Aubrey, they were of course all lost when we were wrecked. I had them all packed in that little box I made from the wreck of the *Leonora* when we were cast away on Strong Island in 1875 [1874], so that box is gone too. . . . In the same box I had $900.00 in English gold, all lost, but a great deal of it found by the natives who won't give it up, and as they are 2000 strong here and we are only 9 all told I will never see that money again. . . . We were likely at first to have lost all our lives by the natives, but our captain's conduct was cool and quiet, and fortunately for us all I found a native who could talk Samoan and although we had one fight on the second day there was no bloodshed, till a native picked up one of my rifles on the beach and as the beach was covered with liquor he also got drunk and shot his own brother dead on the spot in his drunken fury. With the aid of the two Samoan missionaries on the island we have recovered a good deal of stuff that was stolen by the natives, but all of it that belonged to me was some clothes and 16 Enfield rifles and one revolver. We are expecting the *George Noble* here next week and if I do not get a passage by her I can at least send you a letter. . . . There is another thing I want to get to Sydney for; for some time I have been suffering from a poisoned foot and the doctor of the man-of-war could do nothing for it on board but said that it can be cured with ice baths; it is very painful and I have now been bad with it five months, otherwise I am in good health."

VI *"How Does a Bloke Write a Story?"*

Fortunately, Louis was picked up by the *George Noble,* a three-masted trading vessel heading for Sydney. On the way, via Drummond's Island, Tarawa, Makin, and New Caledonia, Becke was privileged to meet the notorious King Apinoka of Apemama. This absolute monarch was also to be described in a memorable passage in *In the South Seas* by Robert Louis Stevenson, written on his cruise in the steamer *Janet Nicol* in 1889, seven years after Becke's encounter. Louis was able to testify that Stevenson's description of the sharp trading propensities of King Apinoka—especially in acquiring firearms with which to wage war on neighboring islands and to punish his own rebellious subjects—was not exaggerated.

The king, "the most famous of all the fat potentates of the mid-Pacific isles,"[18] whose immense girth was clad in a suit of black cloth, wore a white helmet-hat, white canvas shoes, and a network of heavy gold watch chains across his huge paunch. He came aboard the *George Noble* in a whaleboat rowed by ten handsome young women, members of his crowded harem. After a glass of champagne with a dash of brandy, he began asking to trade for rifles. The captain mentioned that Becke had salvaged a fine breechloading shot-gun, and the king bought it for what the skipper privately informed Becke was too low a price. In return, Becke sold the king a shiny spring-balance scale for five times its worth. Apinoka paid out the money in gold with a businesslike air, and tried to hire Becke to serve as his secretary. As the king departed, having sold his copra crop, the captain unknowingly "hurt his feelings" by asking about his favorite wife, a Tarawa girl. A passenger on the ship explained that the girl had been seen speaking to one of the king's young fishermen. Both had been immediately killed by the monarch of Apemama.

Becke waited in Sydney for the offer of a new station, but the letter from Henderson and Macfarlane arrived, ironically, just one day after he had departed to take a dangerous post in cannibal New Britain. Here he became acquainted with the colossal swindle of the South Sea colonization scheme perpetrated by the cynical French master-criminal Charles-Marie-Bonaventure du Breil, Marquis de Rays. His brief account of the venture tallies fairly well with standard versions.[19] His only mention of his part in the affair, however, is the statement that Captain Gustave Rabardy of the immigrant ship *Génil,* usually considered to be a demon only less evil than his stay-at-home master, died at his side. "His dying words to the writer of this sketch, as he grasped his hand for the last time, were, 'I have tried—and failed. I have not one competent officer with me to help me maintain my authority or shoot some of the ruffians who have ruined the expedition.'"[20] No other document has been found linking Becke with Rabardy or the expedition, but his familiarity with the tragedy is plain, and the presence of this young trader at the scene in St. George's Channel on February 16, 1882, might well have gone unremarked.

Becke, as a newcomer, was assigned to the most distant and isolated trading station on New Britain. During his stay the cannibal natives perpetrated some horrible massacres. He also suffered illness, for when he wrote to his mother on November 1, 1882, from Majuro in the Marshalls, he added a postscript that he was "nearly clear of fever."

Louis had escaped from New Britain, but by unpleasant coincidence he had been sent to Majuro by his German employers, Herissheim & Company, to trade in competition with his friends of Henderson & Macfarlane. He hoped after his year was up, though, to get a place with this New Zealand firm. He adds in the letter to his mother: "I am in hopes again of getting something from the Government for the goods plundered from the *Orwell*, as Mr. Carr tells me the island is to be visited by a man-of-war and fined $15,000 or £3000."

Thus it went with the trader's life. Illness and bad luck might strike, but Becke never lost his boyish urge for new scenes. He was honestly fond of the brown men and women of the islands, and had a happy knack of getting their confidence. In this way he stored up his deep knowledge of their languages, customs, and beliefs for future literary use. He also may have served on a German "blackbirding" ship, a trade he seemed to know at first hand.[21]

The pull of the islands for such men as Louis, although homesickness might strike now and then, is rhapsodically voiced in a passage he once wrote about the South Sea traders: "Return? not they! Why should they go back? Here they had all things which are wont to satisfy man here below. A paradise of Eden-like beauty, amid which they wandered day by day all unheeding of the morrow; food, houses, honors, wives, friends, kinsfolk, all provided for them in unstinted abundance, and certain continuity, by the guileless denizens of these fairy isles amid this charmed main. Why—why indeed, should they leave the land of magical delights for the cold climate and still more glacial moral atmosphere of their native land, miscalled home?" [22]

Nevertheless, Becke did return home to Australia, to the very village he had hated as a boy. On February 10, 1886, he sedately married Mary Elizabeth, daughter of Colonel Maunsell of Port Macquarie.[23]

He took his wife to the islands, but like most white women, she suffered a decline there, and within a few years the couple were in Sydney. The slightly built Louis, himself stricken by recurrences of fever, was unable to get a job, except the painful, ill-paid work of grubbing out stumps. Once he tried and failed to raise chickens on a tract infested with chicken-eating snakes.[24]

Unaware that the twenty years of his trader's existence was over, Becke contemplated a return to the islands, even if the life would kill him. He wrote to a firm at Efate in the New Hebrides on October 1, 1892, asking for a station. "I am 35 years of age," he reported (he was actually thirty-seven), "am married (with two children), am well up in all branches of the island trade, a good rough carpenter and used to sail small craft, but cannot navigate. I am also a good bookkeeper and accountant and have very satisfactory references as to my ability and sobriety. . . . I should very much like to return to the islands, either as a trader or in some other capacity, and, if I could, obtain a station where my wife could accompany me." [25]

Had the answer been favorable, Becke and his family would have returned to one of the most lethal groups of islands, "the white man's grave," and he would probably never have written a line of the reminiscent volumes that are treasured today.

Disconsolate, Becke one morning encountered in Pfahlert's Hotel in Wynyard Square the Australian explorer and author, Ernest Favenc, who listened to some of his yarns and said immediately, "You ought to be a writer." He took Louis down to the offices of the Sydney *Bulletin* and introduced him to the celebrated editor, J. F. Archibald.

Eccentric, frail, mercurial, and sardonic, Archibald had a brilliant gift for journalism and as co-founder of the *Bulletin*, always noted for its hospitality to writers of stories of the Australian "outback," was able to attract the loyalty of many talented authors. Later, Becke always paid high tribute to his first editor, who, he said, "taught me the secrets of condensation and simplicity of language." [26] After listening to Becke tell a few tales, Archibald asked him to write something for his columns.

Becke had never written a story. "How does a bloke go about it?" he asked.

"Write just as you are telling me now; they will make dashed good yarns!" advised Archibald. Taking him at his word, Louis Becke went to his scantily furnished room on William Street, and on a table made of gin cases scrawled out half a dozen stories.

The first of these, "'Tis in the Blood," appeared in the *Bulletin* on May 6, 1893. A number of others were accepted, and in 1894, the year of Stevenson's death, Becke's first book, *By Reef and Palm,* a collection of his South Sea tales, was published in London. Thereafter, he was committed to a long voyage on the strange seas of a literary career in many parts of the world, far from the New South Wales of his origin.

CHAPTER 2

Adventures in Europe and Elsewhere

THE stories of Louis Becke were popular with *Bulletin* readers. As a free-lance writer he began selling pieces to various English journals, such as *Pall Mall Gazette, English Illustrated, Sketch, Illustrated London News,* and *New Review.* He was also well received by the Sydney *Evening News* and by *Town and Country,* whose editor, Walter James Jeffery, soon became his collaborator and with whom he was to write half a dozen books. Becke used various pseudonyms, such as "Ula Tula," "Te Matau," and "Papalagi."

But income was still insufficient to support a family. His wife was often ill, and in 1894 a little son died of lockjaw. Becke was never again to have a son.

The same year, a novel by "Rolf Boldrewood" appeared, most of which consisted of material which had been supplied by Becke in 1893 for a small sum and had been incorporated almost without change and completely without acknowledgment. Discussion of this early use of Bully Hayes as a fictional character will be postponed until Chapter 5. But between the time when Becke, still little known himself as a writer, supplied manuscript for another, and the time when he wrote to protest its unfair use, he had become the proud author of a book issued in London by one of the world's leading publishers.

I *Two Noble Dukes Lend a Hand*

Circumstances of the publication in September, 1894, of Becke's first book, which some consider his best, are fairly clear. Archibald, editor of the *Bulletin,* bundled up and sent a number of Becke stories to his friend H. W. Massingham, editor of the London *Daily Chronicle,* who then wrote to the author, in part: "Just a line to tell you of the receipt of your volume of stories, which I have read with the greatest interest. I think them extremely strong —incomparably stronger than Stevenson's work, which seem to me clearly derived from them." Massingham, declining any commission, forwarded the stories to Mr. T. Fisher Unwin with his recommendation.

At that time Unwin (1848–1935)—a name still known today in the British literary world—was one of the leading and most aggressive publishers. He knew a good thing when he saw it; in the same year he was to publish the first books of both Becke and Joseph Conrad. But he wrote to Becke on December 14, 1893: "I look on the publication of your stories as somewhat of a venture, not only from their being by a new writer but from their subject matter, which makes them somewhat venturesome; however, I feel that their power and interest should pull them through."

Unwin enclosed two forms of agreement, one for the outright purchase of the volume and one on royalty terms. Becke, never well off for money, took the offer of cash, reputed to be £65. The price presumably included several more stories he had sent to Massingham later, for Unwin wrote Becke on April 11, 1894: "Besides the stories you originally sent I have taken the other three or four to include in my volume and have increased my first offer and will pay you a larger sum for your work. . . . Your book will be published in a little series of 1/6 books entitled the Autonym Library."

Louis had a bright idea. Why not get the Earl of Pembroke to write an introduction to the book? Although they had never met,[1] the earl might be persuaded to sponsor this effort by a writer of stories about the South Seas through which Pembroke had sailed with pleasure and had himself written a book about.

George Robert Charles, thirteenth Earl of Pembroke, born in 1850, was holder of a title going back to the twelfth century and a descendant of the famed Herbert family. The first of the Herberts to be created earl won the title in 1551. Among the monastery lands given him was Wilton House, a stately home that anybody who has ever visited its beautiful halls must agree is as noted for its architecture as for sheltering literature. Here was living Becke's prospective sponsor, among many reminders of the past. At Wilton, Countess Mary, sister of Sir Philip Sidney, wrote psalms with her brother, and for her his *Arcadia* was composed. The third earl,

William Herbert (1580–1630), was supposed by some to have been the mysterious "Mr. W. H.," the "onlie begetter" of Shakespeare's sonnets. To him and to his brother, at any rate, the First Folio of the bard's plays was dedicated. Shakespeare himself had performed one of them at Wilton before James I. George Herbert, the metaphysical poet, was a member of a collateral branch of the Pembroke family.

With such a background, it was natural that when the thirteenth earl took a cruise in his yacht through the Pacific in 1870, he should write a book. The result was *South Sea Bubbles,* a collaboration by "the Earl and the Doctor"—the latter was Pembroke's companion Dr. G. H. Kingsley. The book told of the various adventures which ended when the *Albatross* was wrecked in the Fiji Group. This volume was widely read, partly because in 1870 fewer yachtsmen were traversing those waters than in later years, and partly because some passages had given offense to the pro-missionary element.

Persuaded to contribute to *By Reef and Palm,* the maiden book by Becke, an introduction based upon autobiographical notes supplied by the author, Pembroke wrote Becke on May 5, 1894: "I have just finished writing your introduction and I hope it may meet on the whole with your approval. It is rather nervous work writing an introduction for a man at such a distance with no possibility of consulting him as to what he wants said or not said. I have made great use of the sketch of your career that you sent me with one of your letters. I have attempted to forestall the criticism that the subject of the tales is too monotonous on the ground of artistic purpose and that there will be more stories dealing with other aspects of South Sea life to follow."

The material supplied to Pembroke was a highly colored account of Becke's adventures, many of which never happened or happened in a different way. No dates were given.[2] The immediate success of *By Reef and Palm* (it went through seven London printings in ten years) did much to spread the Becke legend. Understanding of the real events of his eventful life was not enhanced when as late as 1955 an Australian reprint of the volume included without correction or annotation this original preface.

The success of *By Reef and Palm* and a second collection, *The Ebbing of the Tide* (1895), plunged Becke into plans for living by his pen. Wanderer that he was, he dreamed of escaping from the grind of Sydney journalism and fleeing to London, literary capital of the Empire. Pembroke wrote him an undated letter from Wilton House: "I expect your determination to come home [i.e., to England] and look after your interests here is not an unwise one. . . . I hope to see you if you come to England but I shall have gone back to Germany to go on with my cure in May." Unfortunately, the thirteenth earl died on May 3, 1895.

Becke was quick to write his condolences to the successor, the earl's brother Sidney, who replied from Wilton House on November 3 that his attention had been called to *By Reef and Palm* by his brother and remarked: "I may say that I read the tales in it with the greatest interest." Becke followed up the connection by offering to send some South Sea curios to Wilton House, but his gesture was politely refused, and as it was to turn out, Pembroke would be of little help to Becke when he actually did get to England.

Another noble earl with whom Becke corresponded was able to offer much more assistance. This was Archibald Philip Primrose, fifth Earl of Rosebery (1847–1929). Twenty letters to Becke from this powerful political figure are to be found in the Dixson Library. Becke seems to have enlisted the interest of a fellow author by sending copies of his books to the earl, who as a champion of the British Empire might well take an interest in South Sea stories, and as the lauded biographer of Pitt, Napoleon, and Cromwell might be able to encourage a new arrival from the colonies. Among the letters the first is dated November 4, 1895, and includes the remark: "I was greatly impressed with the weird power of 'By Reef and Palm.' The first story I thought appalling, and the shark story sometimes haunts me; but that is a tribute to your lurid gifts, which are rare." A letter of April 7, 1896, acknowledges receiving *His Native Wife* and looks forward to *The Ebbing of the Tide.* Later he wrote from Spain to give some useful commentary on *A First Fleet Family,* and when Becke arrived in London he was entertained by Rosebery, who remained a helpful friend for some years.

II *A Welcome to the Old Country*

Becke's third book, the novelette *His Native Wife,* was published in Sydney in 1895. In October, Becke and his little daughter Nora took a trip by steamer and overland coach to his birthplace at Port Macquarie. He was determined to concentrate on turning out a mass of literary material that would bring him enough money to pay his passage to London. He labored hard on his own work, and also on three books on which he was collaborating by mail with Walter Jeffery (see Chapter 4), including *The Mutineer,* the story of Captain Bligh, Fletcher Christian, and the *Bounty.* All rights to this novel were sold to Angus & Robertson, foremost Australian publishers, for £250. Becke was getting together a grubstake for his new overseas venture.

Louis worked at Port Macquarie until April, 1896. He then returned to Sydney and on June 9, having borrowed £200 from his editor Archibald, Becke deserted his wife Bessie and quietly eloped to Europe with a young lady named Fanny Sabina Long.[3]

An article in the Melbourne *Free Lance* of June 18 by "Yelwarc," presumably Crawley, does not mention Miss Long in the valedictory. It does give a review of Becke's career to that time, applauds his easy grace in the approved Australian social function of "shouting" a round of drinks, and concludes: "Mr. Becke has but one child, a little girl of eight, who has been his constant companion in all his island wanderings. She is at present on her way 'ome, *en route* to Belgium, to be placed at school with the children of an old island comrade of her distinguished dad's. Becke himself who has during the past week been in Melbourne left for London last Tuesday [June 16]. He goes on a brief business visit in connection with Island trading, and will return to Australia *via* Canada in about five months."

A more lengthy interview appeared in the South Australia *Register* on June 23, where Becke had paid his first visit to Adelaide in mid-month. The reporter, who terms Becke "the Rudyard Kipling of Australia," gives a lengthy account of the author's career, mainly mentioning Bully Hayes, Becke's first ventures into writing, and his recent collaborations with Walter Jeffery. "The beauty of Mr. Becke's stories are [sic] their simplicity and their naturalness—nothing strained, no striving after effect. He says—'I write a story and never rewrite it. I don't take notes but let it unfold itself. Then if when finished it satisfies me I keep it, but if I don't think it good enough I tear it up.' . . . Mr. Becke is just going home on commercial business, having no literary project in view whatever."

Becke's ship reached Gibraltar on July 23, when he wrote Jeffery that he looked forward to getting letters in London and seeing proofs of their book, *The Mutineer.* He arrived in London in mid-August and went to Morley's Hotel in Trafalgar Square. Here he found waiting to welcome him his friend and former trading boss, Tom De Wolf, now a London stock speculator, to whom Becke was to dedicate *Pacific Tales* the following year.[4]

A voluminous interview in the London *Daily News* on August 15 gives a somewhat highly colored picture of the appearance and the British reception of the antipodean author at the start of his London epoch. "His face is tanned a dark brown by years of brazen suns; he has a restless, roving eye; his hair is black streaked with gray; his moustache is heavy; his nose has just an aquiline curve to it; his neck is bit deep with fiery wrinkles; his hands—ah! his hands are enormous for such a slim-built fellow. They look strong enough to crush a cocoanut or a skull. He is a sombre, melancholy man, this Mr. Becke, and when roused I should say that he is well able to take care of himself. . . . I thought I detected just a faint smell of the sea, but it was soon absorbed by blue clouds of that black plug tobacco which these hard-headed ones love to smoke."

After reporting Becke's observations on opportunities in island trading, adventures with Bully Hayes, cannibal feasts, blackbirding, and missionaries, the reviewer ends: "He will doubtless do his best to execute the 'orders' which are flowing in on him. He has a boy's book on the way, and more sketches; and if ever he gives us a faithful account of his life, without purple patches, it will be an entrancing volume. But already he yearns for the seas again, and is making his plans for some extensive trading operations."

Other interviewers and reviewers commented on Becke. His lifelong stammer was imitated: "I knew a m-m-missionary once . . . ." As the celebrated author of *By Reef and Palm,* he was widely welcomed to the heart of the Empire.

At first, Louis was almost as impressed by the leaders of the Old

Country as he would have been by a high talking chief at a Samoan kava-drinking. "I am still a man who has not worn out his welcome as far as England is concerned," he wrote Jeffery on November 25, 1896. "If I had accepted all the invitations I received and drank all the wine pressed on me I should long ago be under old England's sodden sod." He then proudly reported that he had visited Lord Rosebery's country home in Bucks.

Yet perhaps Becke felt that he was not a wandering colonial, but rather an Englishman whose family went back to the Conqueror and who was now coming home to win a new reputation for his clan. Strolling through London wearing one of his specially made white tropical suits and a large Panama hat, with his tanned face and drooping mustache, Louis caused comment and questions. As he headed for the office of his publisher in Adelphi Terrace, he must have recalled that this literary region was built by the Adam brothers on the site of the mansion of his ancestor, Anthony Bek, Baron of Eresby.

The Fleet Street people were glad to greet their Australian colleague, and to "put him up" for their various clubs: Massingham at the Devonshire, and Phil May—who had worked for five years as a cartoonist on the Sydney *Bulletin*—at the Savage Club, where Becke was to be a member for six years. The American author and New York *Times* correspondent Harold Frederic sponsored him at the National Liberal, and Sir Thomas Lauter Brunton at the Savile. The latter also proposed him for the "awe-inspiring distinction" of becoming a temporary honorary member of the Athenaeum.

Dr. Lauter Brunton was treating Louis for eye trouble, which could be incapacitating to a busy author. "I don't know what is wrong with my eyes; they are very dim and misty and exceedingly painful," Becke wrote to Archibald in Sydney. "I told Banjo [Paterson] that I think it was caused by the shock I received on looking in the glass and seeing myself arrayed in Piccadilly costume. I looked like a confidence man waiting at Redfern Station for his bush prey." [5] Becke was especially grateful to Lauter Brunton, who healed his eyes in a few weeks. He went to this fashionable physician with fear and trembling to ask for his bill. "He slapped me on the shoulder, 'Come and dine here tomorrow night. There are some people who I will ask to come, John Collier, Stopford

Brooke, Harry Cust and others—and don't bother your head about my fees; there are none. But don't smoke cigars, my boy. Stick to your pipe if you *must* smoke." [6]

III *Publishers and Pre-Adamite Agents*

The temptation to forsake literature and return to trading in the Pacific faced Becke soon after his arrival in London. "Some very sound business people here wish me to undertake the general management of a large South Sea Island Investment and Trading Company at £1,000 a year," he wrote Jeffery on August 21, 1896. He proudly reported that he was leaving to inspect some steamships that might be purchased for company work. His eyes were still troubling him, however, and "if they get no better and I am to depend upon my pen for the future the outlook is not a promising one. Not that I am doubtful of my success in that line. I am very confident." Becke's eye trouble returned and became a serious handicap, even making it dangerous for him on the street. "I nearly got run over twice today in Cardiff," he wrote Jeffery on August 14, 1897, "and I can't stand the light at all." He reported on the 19th that he might have to go to Germany to see a specialist if his eyes did not improve, which was like "the doctor who tells the dying pauper in the almshouse that he must go to Madeira and take a villa for six months and live well!" But Becke was able on October 15 to write that "My eyes are ever so much better and I can now get along famously but have to use strong glasses."

The business plans finally fell through, probably because of rebellion and war in the Spanish Philippines, and Becke continued writing. His American friend Harold Frederic once tried to get him to meet an influential if slightly shady knight who headed a company that proposed to exploit British New Guinea—a real-life character not too different from the plundering hero of Frederic's posthumous novel *The Market-Place* (1899). Frederic, nowadays highly revered as a turn-of-the-century forerunner of modern disillusioned naturalism, would bellow at Becke as he entered the smoking room of the National Liberal Club and introduce him to friends as the last genuine pirate, saying that both Becke and Bully Hayes had been sentenced to death but that Becke had been spared because of his youth and his agreeing to return to the islands and preach the Gospel. Frederic in a letter of July 6, 1898, from Kenley, Surrey, remarked that Becke's prospective business associate was "also a pirate. He is a fatter and more cheerful buccaneer than you are. . . . Together, you might plunder a hemisphere . . . I'm quite unable to guess which of you would then be most likely to return with the loot as the survivor."[7] But Becke's "feelings" caused him to reject indignantly any connection with such a heartless scheme, which he later exposed in one of his "London Letters" to the Sydney *Evening News*.

Becke's temperament, even so, was always that of the trader, and although such a choice would have been a loss to literature, he might have been happier in a business career. As his daughter Niya wrote to me on December 31, 1963: "We feel Louis Becke should have remained de-civilized. He was very attached to Mother, but the strain of trying to provide for a family by writing was not the solution for a born sea-rover."

"During my first months in London," Becke recalled, "I worked hard all day and frivolled at night. I turned out a lot of magazine stories and was well paid for them."[8] His frivolling included making the acquaintance of many influential men. He dined with the great Rosebery, lunched with Walter Besant, and attended an Omar Khayyam Club dinner at Frascati's Restaurant on November 20, 1896. He several times saw the "dowger" Lady Pembroke, but did not meet the fourteenth earl until later, and the connection was not to turn out as valuable as Becke had hoped.

A. Conan Doyle, creator of Sherlock Holmes, sponsored Becke for the Author's Club. Becke in 1897 accepted an invitation to visit Rudyard Kipling at his home, Bateman's, Burwash, Sussex. Concerning a copy of *By Reef and Palm* which was given him, Kipling remarked that he had read it long ago and "heartily admired" it. To Becke's bread-and-butter note, Kipling replied: "Thank you—but I'd give up 50% of all possible advantages for three months of Christian temperature (84° in the shade) in a hammock and a white suit, with a gin and coconut milk swizzle to follow. Wouldn't you?" On November 7, 1897, Harold Frederic invited Becke to his country place to meet Stephen Crane, and added: "Roast suckling pig on." S. R. Crockett, popular Scottish novelist, wrote friendly letters. Paul Blouët, a successful lecturer who also wrote under the name of "Max O'Rell," invited Becke to a party to meet Mark Twain.[9]

Becke's writing about Pacific geography brought him an additional honor. He was the first Australian, according to his daughter, to become a member of the Royal Geographical Society.

Louis also found time to greet fellow Australians in London. He sat to the left of the guest of honor, Dr. E. C. Stirling of Adelaide, at a dinner given by the *Illustrated London News* on February 25, 1897. When James Tyrrell of Angus & Robertson, later a well-known bookseller and collector in Sydney, arrived with a letter of introduction, Becke gave up a fishing trip with Kipling to meet the visitor in London. Edmund Barton, destined to become the first prime minister of Australia, came to the capital in 1900 to see the Federation Act through the Imperial Parliament, and Becke dined with him and his friends.

The strain of London life upon the man from the Pacific was increasingly harmful. In the autumn of 1896 he had moved to the seaside town of Deal to escape the London weather. "I trust Mrs. Jeffery is well," he wrote to his Sydney collaborator on November 2. "She is lucky to be living in a genial climate, instead of this vile, filthy, smoky, dirty, foggy, ill-smelling, poverty-stricken country."

Becke was collaborating with Jeffery at long distance and taking care of their joint business affairs and worries about serial and book publication. Despite Becke's journalistic success and his publishing of an average of two books a year, he was beset by money troubles. Nora needed an operation that would cost £35—an amount about half the value of outright sale of all book and serial rights to such a volume as *The Ebbing of the Tide*. On the last day of 1896 he wrote to ask Jeffery to lend him £10 to pay his Sydney lawyers.

Louis was still occupied with business in connection with the South Sea company. He wrote from his Thames-side home at Richmond on April 28, 1897, that "I have been simply rushing to and fro over England in connection with this company affair." At about the same time he began using on his notepaper the Becke family crest—a golden peacock with a crown around its neck, with the motto: *Umbrae persequimur umbras*—"We shadows pursue shadows."

Becke had congratulated himself in a letter of August 21, 1896, for having turned over all his manuscripts to the well-known agent A. P. Watt, but complained that T. Fisher Unwin was still trying to get material from him direct. He protested about Unwin's having taken two-thirds of the serial income from *A First Fleet Family,* the first Becke-Jeffery novel, but later accepted a settlement of £100. Despite other irritations, Unwin continued to be Becke's chief publisher through 1906.

Louis soon began voicing doubts about the efficiency of his agent, whom he did not often see and who exasperated him with his "tortoiselike" and "pre-Adamite" ways of doing business in his leisurely Victorian way. The agent did not reply to requests and once lost a manuscript. Several times Becke made sales to editors through his own efforts and paid Watt his ten per cent commission anyway.[10] "I can clearly see that as I now stand in London," he concluded on August 19, 1897, "I can manage my literary affairs better than any agent."

IV *In the Jungles of Jamaica*

He moved from Richmond to Eastbourne in Sussex, to be near the sea, and here were born to Fanny Sabina Long, on October 30, 1897, and September 27, 1898, his two daughters, Alrema and Niya. "It is a pleasant thing to have a mite of a baby girl to love," he wrote fondly to Jeffery on June 21, 1898; "it elevates men like you and I above our sordid daily worries and the continual d—d fight for money."

Becke's health was not improving. He dictated a letter to Jeffery on January 7, 1898, saying: "I am too sick to write you a long letter." On April 14, he was "in downright agony with rheumatic neuralgia." Strangely enough, this man who had lived in the tropics did not badly mind the terribly cold winter of 1897–98 but suffered greatly from the heat of the English summers. On October 11, his illness was so deadly that he wrote to Jeffery: "I am now putting all *my and your affairs in order.*" He added on November 18: "I am fighting against fate—my health is gone nearly altogether; and I am doing all that should be done to put our joint affairs in proper order in case I slip my cable somewhat unexpectedly. . . . *I have sold out the entire copyrights of my own books to Unwin.*" Fortunately, he recovered his health enough to continue to earn money to support a family and to publish twenty-five more books.

Becke had a chance in 1898 to help Massingham get a journalistic *coup* when the rival wide-eyed editor of the *Wide World Magazine* published an article by "Chevalier de Rougemont" which was full of wild South Sea tales and promoted a scheme for selling gold-mining shares. Becke was able to expose the "Chevalier" as one Henri Louis Grin of "Sydney photographic and diving-apparatus fame." In a letter to Jeffery, Becke complained that the promoters accused him of being hired to expose the scheme, but that all he got was his usual space-rates for writing an article in the *Daily Chronicle*.[11]

Around 1900, when Becke had decided to leave England, Joseph Conrad—another sailor who had "swallowed the anchor" and was slaving ashore to support a growing British family—was working in Kent at *le vrai metier de chien*, writing *Lord Jim*. Becke must often have felt like Conrad's Jim: "There was no going back. It was as if I had jumped into a well—into an everlasting deep hole." From now on, writing would be his only source of income.

In 1900 the Becke family moved to Ireland, perhaps to find a spot that was quieter than London and cheaper. Since Louis had sold all his books outright, he had to produce more books and articles, but these could be marketed by mail. The English climate had never agreed with him, but he enjoyed locating at No. 3 Bungalow, Greenore, County Louth—again a residence within sight of the sea.

In the summer of 1902 Becke once more went voyaging. But this time he left a family behind, and his letters home reveal that he was not only "lonely as a bandicoot" much of the time, but was also badly ill and injured part of the time.

Apparently he was given a free round-trip ticket on the Direct Line to Kingston, Jamaica, B.W.I., in the expectation that he would write some publicity for their fine ships. He also wanted a change for his health and an opportunity to finish writing *Helen Adair*. He did enjoy the passage from Liverpool to the Caribbean, and it was a delight to him to see flying fish again.

He landed in Jamaica on August 1, and the agent of the line, who had traveled on the same ship, gave a luncheon in his honor at the Myrtle Bank Hotel. The local newspaper reported that Becke planned to remain for six weeks and had been attracted to the island by reports of the tarpon fishing, a sport in which he hoped to indulge. His intentions were further reported as "partly for the sake of his health, partly for pleasure, and partly for the purpose of securing 'matter' for fresh stories." The interviewer found him "one of the most charming of men. Distinction and success, which turn the heads of many people, have failed to spoil him. He is as natural and artless as the natives of those far-off South Sea islands whose characters he has drawn with such touching sympathy, tender grace, artistic insight, and consummate vividness and fidelity." [12]

The day after his arrival was Emancipation Day, anniversary of the date in 1838 when the slaves had been liberated in the island. He was rushed off to the races, and wrote home that "There was an enormous crowd, whites, blacks, browns, yellows, pale orange, dirty orange, and in fact all hues of skin." [13]

He soon moved out of town to the Constant Springs Hotel, but even there it was too hot for him. He caught a virulent local form of bronchitis which racked his slight frame day and night. His opinion of the island capital was low. "Kingston is a fearful hole—an inferno of heat, dust, coal dust, mud dust, and bad smells," he wrote on August 11. On September 1, when he had just returned from a lengthy tour of the island, he repeated: "Kingston is a perfect hell and is the third hottest city in the world." On the 3rd he mentioned that there was much malarial fever in town, and concluded: "I must say that nothing would induce me to live in Kingston." The previous day a "terrific thunderstorm" had struck. "It reminded me of N. Queensland. There were but two thunderclaps, but each one was really awful, and glass was shattered everywhere. Horses etc. ran away into the bush and laid down and the lightning was something awful."

The visiting literary lion was popular. "I don't know how to evade the many invitations I get," he wrote on August 23. "It really wants all the tact in the world to prevent people quarreling—but I can't go to six places at once." His opinion of the society was not high, as he had expressed it on the 20th. "Every man and every woman has some fishy story or stories about them concerning their moral reputations and I can quite imagine the stories to be true. But I do not wonder at the white men here, married and single, carrying on with the various breeds of yellow, brown, and puce-coloured women when the white ladies set them such a bad example. Their lives seem to be devoted to doing nothing but getting themselves mauled about by swaggering, dissipated soldier men who practically boss Jamaica society and put on immense side."

Becke bought Panama hats for his womenfolk and sent them crates of fruit and a beautifully polished stuffed turtle. But even after adventures in the mountainous jungles of the inland, he was not inclined to linger. Only the previous May, Mount Pelée on the island of Martinique to the east had explosively erupted and killed forty thousand people, and the dust in the atmosphere had affected the weather and brought startling sunsets. "The weather today *is awful,*" Becke wrote on September 18. "People here are beginning to get frightened at the awful things happening at St. Vincent and Martinique, and the sky at night is enough to give one the horrors." He planned to depart on the 23rd, but was delayed for another week.

V *Literature a "Scurvy Paymistress"*

On the morning of September 30, the last day of his stay, Becke suffered an accident that might have put him into the Jamaica hospital, possibly to catch yellow fever and die. He rose at 6 A.M. to pack. To open a window that was stuck, he climbed on a table, overbalanced, and fell on a crate. When he could get his breath he took a cab to a doctor, who said the fall had "deflected two of my ribs and badly strained the muscles of the spine or whatever they are." Horrified to hear that Becke was leaving at 9 for America, he "trussed up" the injured man with tight bandages and warned him that if he were seasick he would kill himself. "It is simply torture when I have to cough or sneeze," the sufferer wrote, but he congratulated himself on escaping a worse plight, and fortunately did not get seasick.

Becke's ship, the American United Fruit steamer *Admiral Sampson,* took only six days to Boston, traveling at 17 knots. He decided that he would immediately board the train for Montreal, where he hoped to get a rest and meet people to whom he had letters of introduction. After thirteen hours on the train, he arrived during a cold spell which felt to him like the dead of winter.

As he recalled later, he laughed a good deal during his short stay, despite his fractured ribs and a recurrence of his bronchitis.

"The students of McGill University gave me a great time. I had letters to the President, Professor Drummond, whose delightful book of verse in the French-Canadian patois 'The Habitant' is known and read throughout the length and breadth of Canada. I met many Australians in the land of the snows and Australian literature was quite prominent in the bookstores. It was savagely cold during my stay in Montreal and the lower streets impassible to vehicular traffic. Every night half a dozen or more students would come to my room to 'keep me company.' Most of them had banjos and we ate Prince Edward Island oysters and drank Guinness's stout until the small hours of the morning. Two waiters were kept going all the time." [14]

Nevertheless, Becke was glad to terminate his trip to the West Indies and Canada. His last letter, posted on the Beaver Line steamer *Lake Champlain* at Trois Rivieres, Quebec Province, on October 10, mentioned his bronchitis and said that "Several times I thought I would die from exhaustion from coughing. . . . I shall be so glad to get home! I have to walk about with a stick as my back hurts me so much."

Becke got back home to Greenore safely. But after the family had spent four years in Ireland, they casually took a steamer to France to enjoy a brief holiday. The visit lasted three and a half years. Nora went to school in Le Havre, and the rest of the family moved here and there in the northern part of the country.

The French period is described in *Sketches from Normandy*, Becke's single volume that does not deal with the Pacific. This was made up of short pieces contributed to the *Westminster Gazette* and *Pall Mall Gazette*, usually under the pseudonym of "Tom Denison." The tone is one of slightly forced humor concerning the minor catastrophes of a British family living in Le Havre or Rouen or on provincial farms, enlivened by the visits of a slangy English youth named Jimmy Potter who gets into and out of international scrapes.

Few autobiographical details are revealed in the book, but one gets at times a feeling of quiet desperation, as when the author, trying to support a wife and three daughters by his driven pen, is cooped up with a bad cold in a Sainte Honorine villa after a week of steady rain, forced to read proofs, write a series of newspaper articles, and finish a book for boys while bickering with the landlady in bad French about a flooded basement and at the same time staving off bill collectors. Other rancors of the literary life include silly queries from publishers' "readers," illustrators who draw Micronesian canoes with sails upside down and outriggers on the wrong side, and Australian bush authoresses who send him bulky, unsolicited manuscripts with postage due.

A valuable recollection by his daughters of this time in Becke's life was sent me by Niya in a letter of December 31, 1963: "My sister and I remember Louis Becke as a man always keenly interested in sailors and the sea; he loved fish and ships and all marine creatures from shrimp to shark, and had a fascinating fund of stories about strange adventures in the South Seas. He owned, in the earlier days of his seafaring life, wonderful fishing tackle and well-oiled and shining rifles, pistols and revolvers, expensive field-glasses, barometer and telescope, and many excellent books. When in the West Indies he played cards once too often and as a result was parted from a lot of coin. As a result of this experience he did not allow cards in our house, and some years later he sold many of his rare and valuable Pacific Island curios and other valuable things."

Becke's financial necessities led him not only to part with precious instruments and books, but also to borrow from friends. His noble patron Lord Rosebery wrote him on January 10, 1904: "I hasten to enclose the cheque you want. It gives me real pleasure to be of service to you and I beg you not to harass yourself about the date of repayment." On the following November 30, the earl wrote in part: "I beg you, as I begged you at the time, not to trouble yourself about that advance. Indeed I think it possible from your letter that you may be under some temporary inconvenience in which I could be of use. If so, please let me know. Write a long autobiographical story with incursions into the South Seas, with plenty of adventure and a Bully Hayes of some kind in it!" Apparently Becke still worried for some time about this or a similar kindness, for as late as April 3, 1907, Rosebery wrote: "I must beg of you not to trouble yourself about the sum I advanced to you. In the mean time I am sorry to hear that you are not getting on better; but literature is always, I fear, a somewhat scurvy paymistress." With this truism, the Rosebery-Becke file in the Dixson Library ends.

VI *Death of a Whale-Hunter*

Broke and ill as he was, it is little to be wondered if the man from the Pacific began dreaming again of his bright islands. On August 28, he wrote to F. W. Craig in New York, stating his intention to settle in Tutuila or Tahiti.[15] As it turned out, he was unable to depart for three more years, but he made plans. The two gazettes that had taken his French sketches were willing to contract for some articles he would write on his journey back to the South Seas. On December 21, 1907, he wrote to Messrs. Burroughs Wellcome, a London pharmaceutical firm, saying that he expected to travel through the Pacific to make a natural history collection and would be glad to furnish them with supplies of kava root and also a quantity of the *at-at* vine, the latter a guaranteed cure "for even the most chronic cases of gonorrhea." [16]

On the following February 17 he obtained a letter of introduction from R. W. Thompson, foreign secretary of the London Missionary Society, stating that Becke purposed "starting on a long tour among the Islands in the course of a few weeks" and commending him to the hospitality of the gospellers whom he had not always treated in admiring fashion in his stories. Another letter from Thompson to Becke said that there was a good German school in Apia, suitable for the education of Becke's daughters. Apparently "Lui" intended to return for some while to his old stamping grounds in Samoa.

At last the family was packed and on its way back to the antipodes, which the two youngest daughters had never seen. An interview was granted the Wellington, N.Z., *Dominion* on September 9, 1908. Louis was now not only a writer but an ethnologist with solid scientific backers. "He is to report to the Royal Geographical Society on the Solomons, will make a collection of the fresh-water fish of the same group for the South Kensington Museum, and make ethnological collections and investigations on behalf of the Berlin [Museum] authorities. . . . The expedition is expected to occupy twenty months or more."

Despite brief hospitalization for a chest complaint, Mrs. Becke recovered and was warmly welcomed by New Zealand friends of her husband and accorded the privilege of "soaping" the big Waimangu geyser at Rotorua.

On October 4 the Fiji *Times* reported that the Becke family had arrived the previous Monday in Suva on the steamer *Navau* "to study the folklore in the Pacific Islands. . . . For the work in hand he is armed with phonograph and gramaphone receivers for collecting verbatim songs and stories and also supplied with, as Mrs. Becke says with a smile, 'quantities of guns and pistols.'" Probably the Beckes were the first people to work in the Pacific making live folklore recordings in the field. "The chief assistance in the present undertaking is to come from Mrs. Becke," the *Times* continues, "whose researches into the old English folklore songs (she has all of Cecil Sharp's music with her) and dances in the Sussex villages have been so successful, and whose entire sympathy with the work in hand is manifest."

Becke's plans broke up soon thereafter, for some unknown reason—one account states that his European financial backer suddenly went insane in Fiji. The family was back in Sydney in 1909. The following year Louis was elected a member of the Royal Society of New South Wales. He continued writing, but now times were harder and the magic was gone. Bad health and more frequent drinking added to his desperation and alienated him from his family. A harsh letter from a friend of happier days says: "I can give you no more money." We shadows pursue shadows!

Recurrent malaria added to the sufferings from rheumatism he had undergone in his Fleet Street days more than a decade before. Although there survives a large newspaper advertisement in which his portrait is accompanied by a testimonial praising Jones' Australian Oil as a sovereign remedy for muscular rheumatism, as well as for occasional bruises and sprains, Louis does not look well in the photograph, although his eyes are as luminous as ever. About this time Norman Lindsay, novelist and artist, described Becke as "a thin, hawk-faced, emaciated man with a ragged, drooping mustache, muffled up in an ulster and speaking with a husky voice that had lost all resonance." Actually, Louis was suffering from cancer of the throat.

For a time he was in a private hospital, but he recovered enough to take up residence alone at the Hotel York, at York and King Streets, indistinguishable from dozens of other Sydney licensed premises. On the morning of February 18, 1913, "at nine o'clock, the housemaid knocked at his door, and, getting no answer, glanced into the room and found Mr. Becke dead in a chair, with the ms. of a short story he was preparing scattered on a table in front of him. He had died in harness." [17]

Once, when recalling his halcyon days in the islands, Becke may have had a premonition of the manner of his death, for he wrote: "Denison [his fictional *alter ego*] often wishes he could live those seven months in Leassé over again, and let this, his latter-day respectability, go hang; because to men like him, respectability means tradesmen's bills, and a deranged liver, and a feeling that he will die on a bed with his boots off, and be pawed about by shabby ghouls smelling of gin." Louis Becke should have died at sea or else have been buried under the palms on one of the golden atolls where he had served as a solitary trader. Instead, he was interred on the following day with a Church of England service in a smug Sydney suburb, attended by his widow, a nephew, and three elder brothers. The grave, at the highest part of Waverley Cemetery, lies not far from those of other fine Australian writers such as Henry Lawson and Henry Kendall, and is carefully tended by those who love Australian literature. There Becke, the boy who dreamed of becoming a pirate and lived to write thirty-five books, lies in a spot overlooking the swells of the sparkling Tasman Sea.[18]

An unsentimental obituary on February 20 in the Sydney *Bulletin,* where Becke had first practised his storyteller's art, concluded: "In his strenuous period his favorite recreation was whale-fishing. It isn't the kind of sport that can be met with every day, but Becke whaled as opportunity offered, and no man can whale much oftener than that."

CHAPTER 3

Tales of a Pacific Trader

BECKE'S shorter fiction deriving from his experiences in the islands of the Pacific contains, it is generally agreed, his best writing. He began his career by contributing to the Sydney *Bulletin,* which specialized in brief, terse, and often harsh yarns of bush life and far adventure, and was taught his trade by a master editor who believed such writing most suited to that time and place.[1]

Naturally, Becke's earliest books are closest to the actual incidents he used as background, and have the charm of freshness and exhilaration. The corollary that only the first three or four books by Becke are worth reading will be shown to be false. True, however, is the idea that one should first approach Louis Becke through his fascinating tales and sketches, which give a better picture than a reader can obtain anywhere else of what life was like among South Sea men and women—brown, black, and white—in the nineteenth century, south of the Tropic of Cancer. For Becke could describe the grubby foreshore of an atoll, or the waters rushing into a lagoon through a break in the reef, or a trader's lonely shack, in such salt-stained and wind-ripped words as to make anyone who knows these scenes cry out in almost anguished recollection, "Ah, that's the way it was!" Becke is the laureate of the prosaic, the curator of the South Seas that swell and roll in the imagination of anyone who suspects that there were serpents even in the paradise of Rousseau and Gauguin.

I *The Sharks of the Tia Kau*

Take as typical a yarn from Becke's first book, *By Reef and Palm* (1894), the one called "A Basket of Breadfruit." It needs fewer than two thousand words to tell and has neither a beginning nor an end, but it immediately drags the reader into island life and for the moment he is a South Sea trader, hurrying his small schooner inside the perilous reef.

It happened in Samoa, at the time when Malietoa was trying to gain control among the warring chiefs. The trader had taken his vessel into Apia and was about to return to his post on another island when he idly stopped to watch a group of native girls chewing kava root and spitting the narcotic juice into the bowl from which toasts would later be drunk.

When he was teased about not having a wife he said that he was ready to take one if a girl could be found who was untouched by scandal; whereupon an old woman presented her beautiful granddaughter. The crowd agreed that she was a girl above reproach, but the maiden was so humiliated by the laughter that she fled, followed by her grandmother.

Some hours later, as he was about to sail off, he was met on the beach by the old woman and the girl, who was solemnly offered to him as a wife, either to marry or to take Samoan style. All the old woman wanted was passage in the boat for herself and her basket of two large, ripe breadfruit.

The trader thought, "This is well for me, for if I get the girl away thus quietly from all her relations I will save much in marriage presents," but during the dark trip he found that he would have escaped giving presents anyway. All the girl's relatives, except her grandmother, had been killed in recent fighting. A day and a half before, her one brother and a cousin were killed, and their heads had been shown at Matautu. Since then she had grieved and wept and eaten nothing.

This news touched the trader and he produced a tin of sardines for a midnight snack, but he could find no biscuit, so instead of ransacking the stores below deck, he decided to cut open one of the old woman's breadfruit. But when he slipped his hand into the basket, under the wrappings his fingers touched a human eye.

Striking a match hurriedly, he peered into the basket and found not breadfruit, but two heads with closed eyes, and white teeth showing through lips blue with death. The old woman had begged the heads from the enemy and was taking them back through the battle lines for ceremonial burial in their ancient village.

The trader was angry at this deception, but the girl explained that Malietoa's troops would shoot them if they tried to run the blockade. Some trick was necessary. That was all. Then the girl ate the sardines and, leaning her head against the trader's bosom, fell asleep.

The incident probably happened, and Becke narrated it with precision, for to anyone who knows Samoa there is an inescapable ring of truth about the setting, the style of expression, and the mood. Island warriors, dusky maidens, running the night blockade in a trading cutter, bundles of breadfruit that turn out to be severed human heads—these are not the imaginings of a fevered escapist but merely the everyday materials of South Sea life, related not for romantic titillation but only something recalled over a pipe on the veranda by the lagoon.

By Reef and Palm contains fourteen tales. The reader who comes to them expecting the contrivances of a Poe or an O. Henry, or the slick, neon-lighted shine of the contemporary magazine story, will need to remember that Becke was not trying to peddle "South Sea stuff" to a jaded audience. He was telling, as simply as possible, of events that nowadays seem melodramatic merely because we live in a different world. The Pacific is no longer a somnolent refuge for Melville's *isolatos* or even Michener's "atoll men." Jet planes run every few days from California to Papeete, luxury steamers unload tourists off Savu Savu and Tin Can Island, and in Becke's native Australia one is more likely to see a Land Rover than a crocodile. Becke's Pacific is gone with the *bêche de mer* trade, the sandalwooders, and the blackbirding labor recruiters. But even today, many of us would prefer to read about the heyday of Bully Hayes and the supercargoes of trading schooners, or about native wives on lonely atolls, than about guided cruises or globetrotters nightclubbing at the Puka Puka Hilton.

Reviews of Becke's first book were on the whole highly favorable. *By Reef and Palm* was printed three times in its first year, was translated into French, went through a number of later editions, and was reprinted in Sydney as late as 1955.

Although the subtitle in some editions is "And Other Stories," it happens that there is no story in the book entitled "By Reef and Palm." The main action of nine of the fourteen stories does deal, as the Earl of Pembroke mentioned in his introduction, with the "loves of white men and brown women," but perhaps "love" is too strong a word for these attachments, which are often casual encounters. Two other stories involve white couples, with native girls in the background; and a third reverses the formula and deals with the deep affection of a half-caste for his native wife, while a white villain lurks on the outskirts. However, although the range of this first book is somewhat limited, the Earl's fear of charges of monotony was unfounded, for there is a fairly wide spread of settings and variety of characterization even in this first collection of short tales.

Aside from "A Basket of Breadfruit," there are more than a few stories that deserve rereading. An early *Bulletin* story written under Archibald's admonitions was "Challis the Doubter," and follows the recipe for pace and simplicity. The climax comes a bit early in the tale, but sentimentality is thus avoided. Challis, who flees from a conventional white wife and is given deep affection by an island girl, is unable even after many months to believe that the values he has found with her can be real. But the island existence is so well pictured as to make it clear early why Challis will decide not to return to the violet-eyed woman "conscious of many admirers and of her own powers of intrigue."

The light tone of " 'Tis in the Blood," about the casual amours of the backsliding convent-taught brown girl Vaega, chosen by a stupid Dutchman who thought to train his future wife, contrasts with the bloodstained chronicle of "The Revenge of Macy O'Shea," with its setting in the Marquesas. The runaway convict's crime of violent hatred against his half-caste wife is told with objectivity and lack of moralizing, for the somber atmosphere and simple drama highlight the characterizations while the language avoids sensationalism. "There be none such as he in these days. But he is now in Hell." There was more than one Macy O'Shea loose in the Pacific in the past century.

For unadorned horror, "The Rangers of the Tia Kau" offers in a few pages a tale that was probably quite true, going back to the time of Becke's voyage between Nanumanga and Nanumea in the Ellice Group. Fortunately, the agony of the native canoe-voyagers marooned on the reef where ranged hundreds of savage sharks "could not have lasted long." This story proved to Douglas Stewart, one of Australia's leading critics, that "no scene of stirring salt-water action was beyond his powers of narration." [2]

II *"The Kipling of the Pacific"*

The strongest love in this volume is that of the half-caste in "Pallou's Taloi." Although we are never taken into the soul of the big, childlike trader Pallou, the dominating emotion of the story is his devotion to his fiery little brown girl. Here is an affection that is, as the Earl says, "exquisitely tender and pathetic," depicted with dignity without departing from actuality or slipping into bathos. The outcome of Pallou's loss is tersely put at the end of the tale: "There's the two graves, over there by that *fetau* tree. Here's his stock-list and bag of cash and keys. Would you mind giving me that pair of rubber sea-boots he left?"

"Enderby's Courtship," in which a triangle is played out in an open boat and among a trio marooned on Ducie Island, seems to indicate that hoggishness is a greater crime than murder. Regardless of the morality, the story—which could so easily drop into melodrama—quickly and surely sketches four characters, including one who does not even appear in the action.

The next two stories are commentaries on the island marriage-market. "Long Charley's Good Little Wife" is won over to wed the trader by three dollars' worth of yard goods. A greater courtship was needed to win Le-jennabon, daughter of the biggest chief on Arno in the Marshall Group, but "The Methodical Mr. Burr of Majuru," whose first wife had left him celibate for ten years, decides that when a visiting buck comes from Ebon and tries to lure away his new wife, he will teach her a gruesome lesson. He beheads the lurking visitor who comes singing "Marriage hides the tricks of lovers," and forces Mrs. Burr to carry the head and sing the song through the village street. Burr, an American by his accent, concludes that this early lesson in fidelity is the luckiest thing that could have occurred. "Ye see, it's given Le-jennabon a good idea of what may happen to her if she ain't mighty correct. And it's riz me a lot in the esteem of the people generally as a man who hez business principles."

"A Truly Great Man" is a grim piece of protocol in the art of setting up a trading station in the Ellice Islands of the premissionary days, when a white man with a musket and a tierce of tobacco could win the chief's friendship and the tribute that "His heart groweth from his loins upwards to his throat."

"The Doctor's Wife" is a parable of the fear of consanguinity among the islanders, and shows the ostracism that the natives could bestow on a white friend who married a first cousin. "The same is the blood, the same is the bone" is the judgment of the dark woman who voices the mores of the tribe. Here Becke does not strive for effect, and the character of the title figure is revealed without stereotype.

One of the more memorable tales is "The Fate of the 'Alida.'" News of the notorious piracy of the Rovique brothers reminds the narrator of the arrival of the *Alida* at Funafuti, which vessel was to take Taplin the trader and his wife Nerida back to her home in the Palau Group. Five years later, when the narrator is supercargo of the *Palestine* under the "smart young American skipper" Pakenham, the whole story of the mutiny and attack by the rascally, lustful lover of Nerida is revealed. The ending of the macabre but realistic account is not unhappy: "I heard that Pakenham had given up the sea, was trading in the Pelew Group, and was permanently married, and that his wife was the only survivor of the ill-fated *Alida*." But Pakenham, who first appears here in the Becke stories, was slated to play a role in many another yarn.

The last two stories in Becke's first book both deal with tragedies of great love, although in differing tones. "The Chilean Bluejacket" is a classic tale of Easter Island, and is prefaced by a sketch of that far speck in the Pacific that has lured and fascinated voyagers since its discovery by Roggeveen. The sad story of the young wife who disguises herself as a sailor and follows her wandering English husband to Easter, only to die when she finds him gone, is told in a series of snapshots involving the views of many observers—natives, naval captains, whalers—who are all bound by common feelings that are barely concealed by the outwardly brusque language. This is one of Becke's finest stories, and will not suffer by comparison with Herman Melville's equally moving tale, "Norfolk Isle and the Chola Widow."

On the other hand, in "Brantly of Vahitahi" the tragedy is unrelieved. The steady downward progress of the handsome young seaman who lost his first command is Conradian in subject, but

Becke's power of condensation makes the faithful Doris and the suicide of Brantly one more commonplace of South Sea existence.

By Reef and Palm has been analyzed in more detail than will be given to the following volumes of tales because it shows the first flowering of Becke's narrative force. Turned out for the Sydney *Bulletin* without benefit of apprenticeship and with only a few offhand bits of advice on the craft, this collection of stories deservedly struck the reading world as that rare thing—innovation. It revealed for the first time the drama and pathos that might be found in the overlooked lives of South Sea traders, sailors, beachcombers, refugees from civilization, domineering white invaders, castaways, and wanderers of the archipelagoes, and their relations with the chiefs, warriors, "half-castes," and maidens of isles flung like small planets across the ocean from the Carolines to Easter Island. Lacking, perhaps, in schooled rhetoric, the narratives never flag, and fail by terseness more often than by being smothered in verbiage. Here were etchings, vivid and precise, of a life limited in range, but one never treated in this way before. Handled by a writer to whom this life had been his own, and who had made it a part of the lives of his readers, *By Reef and Palm* will long hold its niche as the first work of a tale-teller who took his place in Australian literature in 1894. No wonder that the label was immediately fastened upon Becke of the "Rudyard Kipling of the Pacific."

Some even better stories, however, are found in the two volumes that immediately followed *By Reef and Palm*. The next book, frequently bound along with the first, was *The Ebbing of the Tide* (1895). Of it the reviewer in the *National Observer* wrote on May 23, 1896, in part: "Mr. Louis Becke wields a powerful pen, with the additional advantage that he waves it in unfrequented places, and summons up with it the elemental passions of human nature. . . . It will be seen that Mr. Becke is somewhat of the fleshly school, but with a pathos and power not given to the ordinary professors of that school . . . Altogether for those who like stirring stories cast in strange scenes." Another typical review, in the *Sketch* for May 6, noting that the background rendering has improved over that in *By Reef and Palm,* said: "In his brief narratives he stops now long enough to let us see the beauty by the way, to give us a longing to annex and settle down forever on some of the favoured spots he describes—on Pingelap, for instance. There is more atmosphere about the stories; everything is not crowded into the foreground; and, though there is hardly less of the sordid, demoralized European element, the unspoilt native life is more detached and appreciable. Mr. Becke's memory or invention does not easily give out."

III *The Arm of a Lovely Girl*

The Earl of Pembroke had expressed the hope that Becke's later books would include "some of those tales of adventure, and of purely native life and custom, which no one could tell so well as he." In *The Ebbing of the Tide* the range is much wider than that of the first book. Only six of its twenty-one stories deal with the liaisons of white man and brown woman, and the native side of South Sea life is given much more attention. Few of the stories, however, lack at least one white man to give a viewpoint on the native events. And Becke has widened his canvas to cover more tales of the sea, or of the cutting-off of ships, or of wandering souls; several of the tales do not touch the islands at all. He still has not forsaken the somber or bloody, but has offered many more facets of Pacific adventure.

Half a dozen stories at least from *The Ebbing of the Tide* are among Becke's best. One of these is "At a Kava-Drinking." The author's skill here can make the reader feel he is listening over a bowl of kava to a tragic tale of a chief's greed, a white man's pride, and a native's devotion, and even in English words make a speaker sound almost as if he were really talking Samoan, a language that Becke knew well.

"Luliban of the Pool" is a tale of Ponape about "she who dived with one husband and came up with another," narrated by Niya (a name given later to Becke's youngest daughter). The plot concerns the method by which she persuades her ill-tempered white husband, Red-Hair, to challenge her lover, tattooed Harry, to a contest, carrying a stone under water across the pool. The conspiracy of Luliban and Harry, who knew the secret of the cave, results in a gory outcome that seems to be condoned by the villagers.

"Ninia" tells of a half-white girl of Pingelap who with two companions is borne out to sea in a storm, and how after many years is able to return to her mother. The telling is perhaps not well organized, and the reader at first gets the impression that Ninia's white father is the leading character. Harry the American, who with smoking musket herds the terrified natives like beasts, could have been the inspiration for the main figure in Jack London's terrifying South Sea tale "Yah! Yah! Yah!" But the story really most concerns the Christian faith of Ninia's mother and the courage of the three little girls faced with the terrors of a storm, and is convincing and vivid.

Tom Denison, supercargo, who appears in many later stories and one novel as Becke's *alter ego* (sometimes he is called Tom Drake), makes his debut in "A Dead Loss." But here Denison plays a minor role and the main characters are his skipper, Captain Chaplin of the *Indiana,* ex-blackbirder from Honolulu, and Martin the drunken trader, who sells his native sweetheart to Chaplin for five hundred dollars. Chaplin thinks he can get three thousand for her in Honolulu, but when the girl's life comes to a sad end, his five hundred dollars also comes to a sad end. The tone of the entire story is non-committal and typified by a line about Martin's actions: "Pensioning off his other wife, he took the young girl to himself and sold the mother to the local chief for a ton of copra."

"A Tale of a Mask" exemplifies the sharp dealings between a trader who has lost his cash playing poker with Bully Hayes and the supervising Scotch skipper who comes to collect his account. Lannigan the trader plans, when going to the ship to pay his bill, to have his man drop overboard a bag of copper bolts that he is then to claim held a thousand dollars in cash; but when the scheme fails, Lannigan fears that he must save himself in some other way. When the supercargo, wearing a spooky paper mask, tries to scare away a band of natives, Lannigan's loyal wife tells her people to crowd out on the jib-boom, and the vessel runs on the reef. "No one was drowned. . . . But Lannigan had a heavy loss—the bag of copper bolts had gone to the bottom."

"Lupton's Guest" is one of the most haunting of all the tales in this volume. It opens with an evocative paragraph of description of an island lost among the Paumotus, to which Captain Ben Peese—evil crony and rival of Bully Hayes—delivers a conscience-stricken man who seeks peace during the last few months of his life. He finds it in the house of honest Frank Lupton, the trader, and his family. Most impressive is the picture of the native wizard or Snarer of Souls, who senses the crime of the "guest" and offers to save him from the death otherwise foredoomed for that night. He points out two white butterflies hovering outside the death-bed room, and says: "Lo, they are the spirits that await the soul of him who sitteth in thy house. One is the soul of a woman, the other of a man; and their bodies are long ago dust in a far-off land." The stranger refuses the offer and is buried with a carving of a human heart in his hand. Not until much later does Lupton read the clipping that reveals his guest to have been a Californian who had killed his sleeping wife and delivered her freshly cut-out heart to her paramour before killing the guilty man and escaping to Mexico. We are drawn back to ordinary life at the ending, when Lupton says to a new guest: "There's Màmeri calling us to *kaikai*—stewed pigeons. She's a bully old cook; worth her weight in Chile dollars."

The same spirit found in the two earlier books continues in *Pacific Tales* (1897), *Rodman the Boatsteerer* (1898), and *Rídan the Devil* (1899). Of the first of these, the reviewer in the *Westminster Gazette* of July 28, 1897, wrote: "No living author, if we except Mr. Kipling, has so amazing a command of that unhackneyed vitality of phrase that most people call by the name of realism. Whether it is scenery or character or incident that he wishes to depict, the touch is ever so dramatic and vivid that the reader is conscious of a picture and impression that has no parallel save in the records of actual sight and memory."

In *Pacific Tales* the range is wider than in *The Ebbing of the Tide*. Themes and subjects are more varied, and treatments are likewise varied to suit. The tone ranges from the now-familiar grim acceptance of criminality and atrocities perpetuated by white men, through more relaxed reminiscence or sprightly revelation, to the broad comedy of "Mrs. Malleson's Rival." This joking attitude is here new in Becke's collected stories, but the devotion of old Malleson to his pig is an emotion that can be compared with those of other eccentrics and other humorous animals of the South Seas that appear in later tales.

Even the white man and brown woman theme is given a new twist when in "Chester's 'Cross'" we find that the refugee from civilization is really in love with the white woman he left behind, and comic touches are mingled with description of a tragic hurricane that provides the machinery to dispose of the trader's native wife. Cannibalism, as in "The Feast at Pentecost" in *The Ebbing of the Tide*, is treated even more poignantly than before, because in "The Arm of Luno Capal" the victim, instead of being a worthless ruffian, is a lovely and faithful native girl. Other subjects are relatively new—blackbirding, head-pickling, and lost treasure. There is also further attention devoted to the descriptions of islands and to scenes of native life that had been desired by Pembroke a few years before.

IV *Husband-Swapping in the Carolines*

Backgrounds drawn from Becke's Samoan years are shown in such tales as "In a Samoan Village" and "In the Evening," the latter revealing the careless existence that could go on even in Mataafa's stronghold during the civil war. The rivalry of the great powers in those islands is summed up by the answer of a native girl when asked if she would marry a white man: "I would rather have an American; they are not afraid of the Germans." Three studies of Polynesian women appear in "Nikoa," " 'For We Were Friends Always,' " and "The Obstinacy of Mrs. Tatton." We also here meet Alan, the Manihiki half-caste, modeled on a Samoan trading partner of Louis Becke during his early days.

Moreover, we are much further acquainted with Tom Denison, who, briefly appearing in "A Dead Loss," is mentioned in no less than seven stories in *Pacific Tales*. Usually Tom is supercargo under Captain Pakenham, whose first name and ship vary from story to story, but who usually bears Denison's comic derelictions with patience. (Tom was a favorite Christian name with Becke, and Denison, according to tradition, was borrowed from the prominent old fort in the middle of Sydney Harbor, on a tiny island which starving convicts, marooned there for punishment in the old days, nicknamed "Pinchgut." However, the town of Bowen, where Becke spent some time, was formerly "Port Denison.")

Graveyard humor and Becke's enjoyment of Pacific crackpots is shown in "Dr. Ludwig Schwalbe, South Sea Savant." The doctor, a survivor of the Marquis de Rays colony on New Ireland, is unwilling host to an injured sailor who is gradually terrified by the sort of scientific activity indulged in by the doctor. "His collection of skulls, he [the doctor] thought, was about the best ever secured in Oceania, but he deplored the fact of his having had to reject two out of every four offered to him, the crude and inartistic manner in which they had been damaged by heavy iron-wood clubs when their original owners were in the flesh seriously depreciating their value, if not rendering them utterly useless as specimens." And the doctor does not stop at merely collecting heads cured by clumsy natives.

The disdain of Becke's narrators for the missionized native had been evident in "Kennedy the Boatsteerer" in *The Ebbing of the Tide*, in which the islanders were said to degenerate after the arrival of the Gospel: "To them it is a good thing to get half a dollar from the white trader for a sick fowl—which, when bought, will be claimed by another native, who will have the white man fined two dollars for buying stolen property. . . . For instance, the truly unctuous native Christian may ask a dollar for two fowls, but he will also lease out his wife for a similar amount. . . . And for a dollar the native 'Christian' can all but pay for a nicely bound Bible, printed in the Samoan tongue, and thus, no doubt, out of evil would come good." In *Pacific Tales*, "The Old Beachcombing Days," set (as is "The Shadows of the Dead") on the island of Kusaie where young Louis Becke had been marooned for six months, is a strong indictment of the "native preacher"—here represented by Brother Purity Lakolalai, formerly a runaway Kusaie slave who had been converted in Honolulu. The crisis comes in a confrontation between King Togusa and Lakolalai, *protégé* of the Reverend Gilead Bawl from Boston. Practical theology is tested to the utmost when the old king says: "Take thou thy spear, Sikra, and thrust it through this man's body. And if he lives, then shall I believe that he will live forever."

Perhaps the strongest chronicle in *Pacific Tales* is "Prescott of Nauru." It reads not like a contrived, structured short story but a recollection of an actual ex-convict who might have become a legend in his own time because of his unremitting and unrepentant brutality over the years. "No," he can confess, "I'm not a white man. The cat took all the white man out of me at Port Arthur; and fifty years I have lived with kanakas, and I am a kanaka now, body and soul."

A different person, and no less of a type, is "Collier the Blackbirder," a humane man haunted by the memory of a deed he had been forced to commit during a native uprising. Becke's power of compression is here at its peak and he can evoke an atmosphere with a few simple, unpremeditated words, colloquial and vivid. In a few other words he can portray the "trader in goods no longer saleable," and the horrors of the recruiting days when the chiefs sold their people and drove them with shark-tooth swords into the blackbirders' whaleboats until the vessels were splashed with blood from stem to stern. The pace of the climax, when the ship is taken over by its cargo of screaming Beru Islanders, who kill all but Collier and the two men and girls from Aitutaki, is tense. The effect of an exploding powder-keg among the survivors of the massacre is not overly dwelt upon, nor the fate of those remaining Gilbertese who jump overboard to swim six miles back to Beru. Within half a dozen pages we become acquainted with the heart of Collier and feel that in his lifetime such things really could happen to a well-intentioned young sailor.

The volume *Rodman the Boatsteerer* contains many another story that would repay analysis, but only a few will be mentioned. The settings still range widely over the whole Pacific, but perhaps as a concession to female Victorian taste, the book includes more love stories, and even some weak sentimentality now and again. Fugitives from justice, like those in "Ema the Half-Blood," "The Escapee," and "In the King's Service," are not whole-hearted evildoers like Prescott but are sympathetic figures seeking to lead upright lives in seclusion. But such a matter-of-fact tale of the gory old days as "The Cutting-Off of the *Queen Charlotte*" is a reminder that Becke has not lost the touch of realistic, almost historical, narrative of freebooting natives and scenes of massacre.

Denison appears again in the tale of "A Point of Theology on Maduro," set in the Marshall Group. The plot is complex enough to satisfy the modern taste and rises to a climax. What seems to be an amusing clash between the native preacher Lilo from Hawaii and MacPherson, Scottish trader and expounder of Presbyterianism, turns into a battle when MacPherson charitably takes in Rimé, an old Maduro native, who had become converted to Catholicism in Tahiti and had wandered back home with his little granddaughter. The trader is threatened with boycott if he does not eject the "Katolikos," and MacPherson asks the aid of Denison and Pakenham to argue the case in open meeting, for: "The silly auld fule of a Rimé won't give in, and I canna see him starve —the damned auld Papist." The free-for-all that follows the theological discussion is funny, but the aftermath comes as close to tragedy as Becke permits himself.

By now the white lady has taken precedence over the brown woman, and only half a dozen stories in *Rodman the Boatsteerer* deal with native or half-caste girls, who are not highly prominent. On the other hand, amusing questions of island etiquette, which often give etchings of trading life and village psychology, are portrayed in such stories as "Leassé" and "A Ponapean Convenance." In the latter of these the trader's wife sensibly suggests that she and the Yankee missionary's wife should swap husbands for a few days.

V *Shameless Little Salomé*

The best story in *Rodman* is the last one, "The Trouble with Jinaban," also set in the Western Carolines. Palmer, trader on Las Matelotas, for two years has sought to kill Jinaban, violent chief who went berserk and killed a score of his own people. Unable to track the outlaw with whom he has a blood feud, Palmer enlists the help of Frank Porter, a half-Maori sailor, who by a cunning plan captures the miscreant in his lagoon hiding-place. But when the time comes to execute the bloodstained chief, not one of his own people, injured as they have been by his depredations, can face his eyes, and again the raw courage of Porter, who had been sole survivor of an attempt to capture his ship by cannibals, must be called upon to rid the community of evil. "The Trouble with Jinaban" is one of the all-time classics of South Sea fiction.

The reviewer of *Rídan the Devil* in *Literature* for June 3, 1900, concludes: "At his best Mr. Becke tells a story or relates an experience with a vigour and finish that are admirable, and in some half-dozen tales of the present collection he is at his best." In *Rídan the Devil,* Becke started his custom of presenting volumes in which stories and non-fiction sketches and reminiscences were intermingled. His thoughts as the century ended were turning more and more toward his native Australia, and in this book are found both stories and sketches of that country (these will be mentioned in Chapter 6). Denison appears in two stories, both set in Australia.

Of the Pacific yarns, the title story is by far the best, and Rídan will stand up by comparison with Jinaban as a sample of the barbaric courage of the islander. But Rídan, unlike Jinaban, devil and wizard that he is, also has a soul to be saved. A castaway desperate to return to his tiny atoll off New Guinea, Rídan, even though in irons in the calaboose, had strangled a fellow worker on the Samoan plantation for insulting him. Judged incorrigible despite various floggings for trying to escape, he is taken back to the fields lashed hand and foot, and to save him from dying, one of the Samoan crew, Pulu, is kind to him. Even a "devil" has a memory; and the revelation of the sacrifice Rídan makes when the whaleboat overturns while running the reef off Choiseul Island bears close comparison with the artistry of Jack London's ending of his story "The Heathen."

Three volumes containing Pacific short stories appeared in 1901. From *The Tapu of Banderah,* some items of which were written with Walter J. Jeffery (see Chapter 4), the best of the stories that are the work of Becke alone is "Pâkía." A philosophical old Polynesian who has returned to Nukufetau reminisces of his adventures around the world, and of his vengeance on a false sweetheart in Liverpool, in far Peretania.

Yorke the Adventurer has little of note in the way of short stories except for another Denison tale, "Old Mary." Third of the 1901 crop is *By Rock and Pool.* Probably the best of this lot is "Solepa," with its Nukufetau setting and its narrator again old Pâkía, but the story deals with the wild old days on Ponape and the relations between white and brown.

Those who had feared that Louis Becke could not write another broadly comic story, though, were pleasantly surprised with the appearance in *By Rock and Pool* of "Mrs. MacLaggan's Billy," a Denison story set in Samoa, where Becke had worked for the well-known Mrs. Macfarlane. "Billy was Mrs. Molly's male goat, and as notorious in Samoa as Bully Hayes himself." All the mischief that could possibly be exploded by a belligerent, drunken goat on the rampage is compacted into this uproarious yarn. A sequel, telling what happened when Billy was taken to sea in Bully Hayes's brig to fight a duel at Levuka is found in "Billy MacLaggan and the Fiji Ram" in *Under Tropic Skies,* which appeared in 1905.

Several Pacific stories are worth noting in this latter volume, which proves that, although Becke was now living in France, his command over the South Sea story had not waned. The best of these is perhaps "The Awful Duel on Utuān," which shows again that Becke did not lack a sense of broad fun. The period is the aftermath of the ghastly collapse of the gigantic colonization hoax of the Marquis de Rays in New Ireland. The story sounds like history, for Tom Farrell actually was the plantation owner on New Britain who had gone to the assistance of the European "ladies and gentlemen," passengers on the ill-fated *Génil,* who had survived the debacle. It is debatable whether or not Farrell actually told them: "Look here, you fellows, I'll take two hundred of you over to my station, and let you stay there until I can send you to Sydney—or Hades. But you'll have to live on board the steamer, and if you try on any monkey tricks with me, I and my niggers will murder the lot of you." When two of the gentlemen decide to settle an affair of the heart on the duelling field, Farrell sends along a grave-digging crew that dampens the ardor of the would-be killers, but one of them is nevertheless felled on the field of honor. The story strongly implies the impatience of the Pacific frontier with the ridiculous niceties of the code duello vs. knock-down fisticuffs.

Notes from My South Sea Log appeared in 1906. A long review in the London *Times* concluded: "His book must be placed with *Typee* and *Omoo*, and the *Island Nights' Entertainments,* as one of the guide-books to the isles of bliss." Despite the title, *Notes* contains fiction, and some of Becke's best. Such tales as "Waters the Loafer," "The Unknown Ship of Maduro Lagoon," and "Captain Kelly of the *Milly*" range from New Britain to the Marshalls to Samoa, and portray once more the seafaring and island-dwelling types that Becke knew so well. Samoa is the setting for the best story in this book, "By Order of the King." During the time when King Malietoa, favored by the British and Americans, was trying to arm his warriors against the encroachments of the Germans, whose supporters were secretly being supplied with rifles and ammunition from Hamburg, the smart young supercargo of the *Venus,* laden with breechloading new weapons as well as sorely needed provisions, makes a deal with the corps of consuls who are trying to maintain peace during the civil war. He will sell them the provisions they need if they will permit him to store the weapons in the Apia town jail until his companion vessel can pick them up. Of course, Malietoa has secretly paid their price, and when his forces burglarize the jail the next night, all the cases of arms and cartridges make their way to the defenders of Malietoa's lines.

" 'Salomé, the Shameless' " is a bitter blast against the rule of Catholicism on some islands of French Oceania, where a waif of a Samoan girl could receive thirty lashes and then be thrown into a pigpen because she would not abjure her Protestant faith. Such a story reminds one of the regime of the mad Father Laval of Mangareva.

VI *Tom Denison's Last Bar of Soap*

Notes from My South Sea Log also contains one of the most perfect comic stories on the Becke bookshelf, "Saunderson and the Devil-Fish." This character, who had earlier appeared in "Saunderson and the Dynamite" in *Chinkie's Flat,* is a boresome, know-it-all ignoramus who, representing the owners of the *Palestine,* interferes continually with the affairs of Tom Denison, supercargo, and makes the air hideous by playing hymns on his harmonium. Despite being taught a few salutary lessons, Saunderson, desiring to show off before a group of missionary friends in a Gilbertese lagoon, attempts to harpoon the mate of a giant manta ray killed the day before. Of course he fails to strike properly and falls overboard, but the line fouls and the beast leaps across the lagoon in a mad attempt to free herself. "No doubt her passions were aroused, and when her great goggle eyes discerned right ahead of her a boat-load of people, the creature went for it with righteous indignation and deadly intent. Folding her great batlike wings under her body, she humped herself into the shape of an outspread, but submerged umbrella, and then, with a torrent of foam pouring from all round her, she leapt into the air, flattened out, and fell with a sickening crash upon the boat-load of missionaries and Saunderson's harmonium. Then, still dragging the line, she made off to sea, feeling that she had done her duty and got even with the people who had killed her husband and insulted herself." In bed with a fractured rib, remorseful at almost causing the deaths of eleven people, and owing Denison twelve pounds, Saunderson is properly chastened—until the next time.

The Call of the South (1908) shows few signs of flagging powers. The *Daily Telegraph* reviewer remarked of it: "Through all the records of these vicissitudes of fortune, the same vigorous manliness and the same keen eye for a situation are conspicuously present." The *Daily News* added: "We do not wish to disparage the modern novel, but it is within the mark to say that, after a prolonged dose of fiction, Mr. Becke's volume comes as a bracing and refreshing draught."

In *The Call of the South,* "The Man Who Knew Everything" is another sort of Saunderson, a young Britisher who, interested in island sports, refuses to take advice from anyone, becoming angry and remarking that "he had found that all white men who had lived in foreign countries for a few years accepted the rubbishy dictum of natives regarding sporting matters of any kind as infallible." The setting is again the Samoan civil war, and while crossing the lines of the rebel troops Marchmont makes an insulting offer to buy some mascot birds and ends up on the floor, nearly killed by a smash on the side of the head from one of the young chiefs. Efforts to teach him sense lead to one crisis after another, and the final one comes when he decides to paddle out alone at night in shark-ridden Apia harbor in a small canoe to seek the giant *la'heu* fish.

This story from a 1908 volume, along with others such as "Vanaki, the Strong Swimmer," "Kala-hoi, the Net-maker," and "A Bit of Good Luck," will stand up under comparison with those published a decade earlier, although by now the demand for "Louis Becke stuff" was not so great in the London magazines as it once had been.

In the same year, he published *The Pearl Divers of Roncador Reef,* which contains at least three more tales that could well be included in any Becke anthology. "A Blackbirding Incident," for example, is a tricky tale of double-dealing, in which a German labor-recruiter captain bribes an officer of the *Cyprus,* a rival ship, to run it on a reef and forestall the loading of "blackbirds" at the Gilbert island of Butaritari. But the narrator hears of the plot through his friend, steward of the *Kaspar.* The traitorous second mate of the *Cyprus* is marooned on Pukapuka and the ship secretly waits outside the lagoon until the *Kaspar* has loaded nearly two hundred "recruits" and sets sail for the hated German plantations of Samoa. Then, without bloodshed, the Gilbertese under their chief's orders overpower the Germans and swim aboard the *Cyprus,* leaving the greedy Captain Baum outsmarted. "And then, as the *Cyprus* gathered way on her, we all, white men and brown, gave the cheer of the old *Bounty* mutineers when they set Bligh adrift: 'Hurrah for Tahiti!' "

In "The *Manurua* and the *Marguerite,*" the young narrator goes into partnership with a retired whaling captain to make a voyage in the *Manurua* to Arrecifos or Providence Island to catch sharks, whose dried fins and tails bring more than $300 a ton in Honolulu. Then a rival Greek ship sails into the lagoon, fires on the ship, burns the huts ashore, and destroys equipment and provisions. After an exchange of cannon shots the crew of the *Marguerite* haul off and set up a camp on an island, but the crew of the *Manurua* decide not to be driven off by this gang of cutthroats. The enemy boats are dynamited, so that they cannot attack the smaller *Manurua* at night. "We were but seventeen men opposed to over fifty desperate scoundrels, who would have had no hesitation in capturing the *Manurua,* and slaughtering everyone on board if they could do so by surprise. . . . In those wild days there was no law in the South Seas, except in the older settled groups, and the disappearance of the *Manurua* and her company would have aroused but little or no interest—such things were common." The way in which the partners and their mate, who had been a Confederate gunner in our Civil War, fight their duel would have won the admiration of C. S. Forester's redoubtable Captain Horatio Hornblower.

The title of another story, "Nerida, the Maid of Suwarrow," might suggest a sentimental Victorian love tale. But Nerida, daughter of an English captain and a beautiful Portuguese half-caste, is no frail flower. When she goes with her father to salvage the cargo of a sunken pearl-shelling vessel in the lagoon of Suwarrow, or Suvorov, Island, and their vessel is captured by mutineers led by two evil divers who had almost killed her father, the maiden shows that she is not one to lapse into the megrims. "When within fifty yards of the beach," she tells her rescuers, "Musgrave again stood up, and as he did so, I fired and shot him through the stomach; then I quickly shot the three others in succession. Fillis twice fired his pistol at me, and then fell into the water, and I saw the sharks tear him asunder. The noise of the firing awakened my father, and he crawled to the door and watched me empty the two Winchesters into the bodies of the three men lying on the raft, until they were riddled through and through."

It is true that *'Neath Austral Skies* (1909), containing both fiction and sketches, holds few pieces that are vintage Becke (one, "George the Docker," is set in France). But even *Bully Hayes, Buccaneer,* the posthumous volume of stories collected hurriedly and published in Sydney the year Becke died, shows no great falling off of his power to tell a rousing tale, such as "A Bar of Common Soap." Again Denison is the protagonist, and this time he has salvaged a hundred cases of soap which have attained marvellous lather-making properties through having been three months under salt water in a wreck and six months drying out on a tropical isle. The price offered him rises to two dollars a bar, and during the time he has set up on Mangareva as a trader in rivalry with the murderous Rasch, who represents the German enterprises, he has decided to make his fortune by selling the secret recipe to the British soap-making firms, who can then ruin the German competition all over the South Seas. The fate of the last surviving bar of soap during a deadly scuffle is as fine a sample of dramatic irony as anything else in Becke's repertory over the previous twenty years. One who still clings to the myth that only the first few of Becke's story collections are his best should reread his later volumes.

VII *Realist in a Romantic Ocean*

As a storyteller of the Pacific islands, then, Louis Becke can hold his own against any other writer of his time. As Douglas Stewart concludes: "He did have the instinctive understanding that a story should be an interesting tale, not just a fragment of glittering prose; and he did set down, with the most pleasant savor of palm trees, surf, sunshine, and nut-brown maidens, his far-off, romantic, and wicked world of the islands." [3]

Becke's themes are usually simple but avoid moralizing. His characters are also rather simple, as befits the setting in the South

Pacific. H. M. Green, who devotes several pages to Becke's short stories, states: "As the stories appear true, so the characters appear real, so far as they go, but they never go very far. Becke is an exceedingly sharp observer of men and women and actions: he makes them lifelike, and he shows us the simple and various motives that lie behind the actions, but he leaves it at that: there is no question of psychological analysis. . . . His pictures of people or places are full of life and color, but they are all painted from without: he cannot, as A. G. Stephens says, get inside the reader's head." [4]

Becke's heroes and villains, although sometimes natives, are usually white men caught up in tropic life—traders, sailors, naval men, beachcombers, escapists, wanderers, missionaries, adventurers. Though not many of the stories deal with sentimental love affairs, and many of the men take native wives in matter-of-fact fashion, liaisons often last for many years and fidelity is not uncommon.

A number of Becke's heroes have fled a more stable society because they have become black sheep or criminals, and in the islands they often face new problems of violence and survival. It is a rare story that does not include some extraordinary outburst of passion, which is reported in commonplace phrases. But even when it is a woman who commits murder or suffers tragedy, no effort is made to pump up pathos. Somebody kills somebody, and that is that. No effects of horror or regret remain; people died like this in the nineteenth-century Pacific, and there is no use dwelling on the Aristotelian aspects of their fates.

The typical island man of Louis Becke, hero or villain, is not a philosopher, not a poet, nor a tragic figure, nor a visionary or empire-builder. He is usually an average fellow, seeking to make a living or to keep on living, among the challenges of a wild and violent ocean. No time is wasted in psychological probing; we are plunged into the middle of an action and recognize most of the personages at a glance for what they are.

The Pacific setting and resulting cast of characters naturally limit the plot effects that can be achieved, and it is true that the monotony feared by the Earl of Pembroke results when one reads several volumes of Becke's South Sea tales one after another. A frequent criticism likewise is that they are plotless in the technical sense, but one is more inclined to agree again with H. M. Green: "Plot is almost everything with Becke: indeed, some of his stories are mere anecdotes; and the simplicity of the vital rhythms with which he has to deal admits only of plots of certain kinds. . . . He is never at a loss for a dramatic climax; indeed his climaxes appear perhaps a little too regularly, so that about some of them there is a slightly mechanical air." [5]

Becke's style is unchangingly straightforward, imitable, and abrupt, although now and again his evocation of an island scene verges on the poetic. He had trouble at first with dialect, and in such an early story as "Long Charley's Good Little Wife" he mingles in one paragraph British slang, *bêche-de-mer* pidgin, native words with translations in parentheses, and a kind of Biblical diction that is supposed to sound like a translation from the Polynesian. Later he was able to avoid these grotesque mixtures, but the problem of giving the effect of foreign speech without cluttering the page with italics and footnotes remained with him, as it did with Kipling and most of the other local-color writers; and a certain leeway must always be granted in representing the words of a non-English speaker, if a sense of scene is required.

But accepting Becke's limited range, he stands out as the acknowledged master of the short tale of life in the South Seas during the past century. He has real power, but it is deceptive. The newcomer to Becke—even if the best works are selected for him—may be thrown off balance if he has formed his ideals on the great Russian, French, or American craftsmen of the modern short story. Becke's artlessness seems innocent. He starts a story: "I stayed once at Rotoava—in the Low Archipelago, Eastern Polynesia—while suffering from injuries received in a boating accident one wild night. . . ." Then with surprising speed Becke involves the reader in a situation which calls forth emotion and partisanship. With apparent bareness he brings on his climax, adds a down-to-earth comment, and the yarn is over. But when the reader thinks back upon this adventure, he acknowledges that in some strange way Becke has conveyed a realistic sense of the island setting, a feeling of dreadful awareness of the plight of the characters involved, and a lasting appreciation of the amazingly varied life of the Pacific as it used to be.

CHAPTER 4

Adventures in Collaboration

REAL collaboration on works of fiction is rare, and seldom continues over a long period. One can recall only a few instances. Mark Twain and Charles Dudley Warner wrote *The Gilded Age* in collaboration in 1873. Joseph Conrad and Ford Madox Ford created *Romance* in 1903. Sir Walter Besant, one of Becke's London friends, was noted for his novels written with a young lady.

The Pacific, for some reason, has been a congenial area for collaborative effort. It is hard enough for one person to write a satisfying novel; when two imaginations must work in harness, the difficulties are at least trebled. Yet Robert Louis Stevenson wrote two Pacific novels—*The Wrecker* (1892) and *The Ebb-Tide* (1894)—with his step-son, Lloyd Osbourne. William Lederer and Eugene Burdick together wrote *The Ugly American* (1958). Over the years Charles Nordhoff and James Norman Hall placed their names jointly on the covers of no less than eleven volumes, including the famed *Bounty* trilogy. And, as will be shown, it is quite possible that, had Nordhoff and Hall ever heard of a novel written by Louis Becke and Walter J. Jeffery called *The Mutineer* (1898), they would have never embarked on their fine trilogy (*Mutiny on the "Bounty,"* 1932; *Men Against the Sea*, 1934; and *Pitcairn's Island*, 1934).

I *Family in an Open Boat*

Over a period of five years, Becke and Jeffery collaborated on three novels, an historical volume, a naval biography, and a book of mingled stories and sketches, *The Tapu of Banderah*. Some uncollected articles also bear their names. Becke while in London was active not only in collaborating with Jeffery in Australia but served as their common business agent, and even went to considerable effort to obtain publication for an historical novel that Jeffery had written on his own.

The relationship was friendly through all that period, as is evident to any reader of a collection of 351 letters from Becke to Jeffery during those five years. Jeffery's influence on Becke should not be overlooked. Much of the historical research for the six books by these two Australians was done in Sydney by the junior author. Never did Becke by himself produce historical novels or lengthy biographies; most of his writing was in a sense either personal reminiscence or the retelling of tales he had heard. It is quite likely that Becke's skill in plotting longer works was improved by his association with Jeffery; even though the *Bounty* story naturally shapes itself, the tight structure of *The Mutineers* was undoubtedly the work of Jeffery in the first draft.

Walter James Jeffery was born on August 20, 1861, at the British base of Portsmouth, son of a retired naval captain. The lad entered the Royal Navy at the age of fifteen, and after two years shifted to the merchant marine. He made several voyages to India and one to Australia, which was to become his home. He then worked on a lightship, a London fire brigade, and a Hampshire farm before returning to Australia, to labor in the Illawarra coalfields. In 1887 he became a reporter on the Sydney *Evening News*, and spent the rest of his life on its staff.

From 1893 to 1906, the years when he knew Becke and worked with him, Jeffery was editor of *Town and Country Journal*, but still had time to delve into libraries and logbooks. He edited the Sydney *Evening News* from 1906 until his death in 1922. At the start of his first collaboration with Becke he was a man of thirty-five. He later spent much time in the Mitchell Library in Sydney (opened 1910), of which he was a trustee. He led in obtaining funds for the statue of Admiral Phillip in the Botanical Garden fronting that famous library, and also caused the reclaiming of the anchor of H.M.S. *Sirius*, Australia's first ship, from the waters off Norfolk Island. Jeffery was independently author of *A Century of Our Sea Story*, which appeared in *The Commonwealth: An Annual* (London, 1900).

Jeffery clearly enjoyed his research and the drafting of books and articles to be rewritten by his friend who was publishing successfully in London and America. He must have been satisfied with the additional income, however slight at times, that came from a half share in their collaborative publications, for there is no evidence that he ever protested to Becke about financial returns.

Theirs was not the sort of two-way collaboration in which each partner rewrites the other's drafts freely until both are satisfied. Exchanging manuscripts between Sydney and London took ten weeks, and hence the burden of rewriting fell altogether upon Becke. Jeffery would send a rough draft of a story or a mass of notes on historical data, and Becke would "work it up" and add the proper amounts of gore, gusto, and romantic passion to satisfy the cravings of their Victorian readership. Sometimes Becke confessed that he could do little to improve on the first draft, but as will be seen, often he added a great deal to the interest of the style.

Since no manuscripts have survived, one cannot extricate all the contributions of either author to most of their published efforts. One of the first reviewers of *The Mutineer* felt confident that he could do so: "There is a good deal of Mr. Becke's overpowering bloodthirst in the course of it. Here we recognize the hand, as well as the pictures of native women and manners. We may ascribe to Mr. Jeffery the historical research which has made the framework of the king's ships, the actual personages of her crew who took part in the mutiny, and the stages of the unhappy foreshadowing of Tennyson's experiment in Locksley Hall." [1]

We are, though, able to examine the body of work done by Becke without Jeffery, and to conclude that Jeffery was indeed more of a historical and biographical author than a spinner of romance. However, at least once, Jeffery wrote a novel on his own. This was called *The King's Yard: a Tale of Old Portsmouth*, set in the period of the American Revolution. Admiral Howe is one of the characters, as is "Jack the Painter," who led a mob that burned buildings in the Portsmouth Dockyard where Jeffery had been born. For many months Becke tried to find a publisher for it, and succeeded in getting it run as a serial in the weekly Portsmouth *Times*. He then pasted up the clipped installments and mailed the result to the agent J. B. Pinker, on March 12, 1901, at which time he wrote to Jeffery: "I should have liked to have altered it here and there, but of course would not presume." The book was finally published by Everett in 1903, and from this little-known story one may judge the fictional powers of Jeffery unmedicated by Becke.

Their first collaboration was an historical novel, *A First Fleet Family,* much of which was based on an actual episode early in the settlement of the convict colony at Sydney Cove. One source states that this was "almost entirely the work of Jeffery." [2]

The "First Fleet" was the name given to the group of convict ships which, in January, 1788, began the settlement that today is the largest city in Australia. The adventures of Mary Broad, the heroine, are well attested.[3] She was transported for seven years for stealing a cloak (a hanging offense in those iron days), and had married William Bryant right after their landing at "Botany Bay." He had been sent there for "interrupting some revenue officers in the execution of their duty"—a euphemism for smuggling. After three years, although they had two children, they feared starvation and exile so much that they determined to escape from Australia. They pooled their money with seven other convicts and secretly bought, from a wandering Dutch schooner captain, some provisions and a six-oared boat, with a lug-sail, a quadrant, and a compass. On the night of March 28, 1791, with their two children—a girl three years old and a boy an infant in arms—the Bryants and their fellow convicts set out to sail to Timor over a course that only Captain Cook had previously followed. They had chosen the worst part of the year, for April is the cyclone season on the Great Barrier Reef.

During their ten-week odyssey, the people in their open boat discovered some geographical features that Cook had missed, such as Newcastle Harbour, later the site of coal-mining operations, where the drenched voyagers warmed themselves with "a quantity of fine burning coal." They also penetrated Moreton Bay, beside which rises the modern city of Brisbane. Despite battles with natives and the perils of voyaging in a small craft through the Great Barrier Reef and across the seas between Australia and New Guinea, the suffering party reached the island of Timor without the loss of a life.

For a while the Dutch governor at Timor believed their story that they were survivors of a British shipwreck, until he overheard one of their number babbling in his cups about the old convict days. The governor then held them all until the timely arrival of

Captain Edward Edwards, survivor of the wreck of his own vessel *Pandora,* while on its way back to England with some captured mutineers from the *Bounty.*

II *Bligh, Christian, and Pitcairn's Island*

On the return to England, in the clutches of Edwards, Bryant and both his children perished, along with three of the male convicts. Mary Bryant survived to stand trial. Her great resolution in urging on the boat voyagers during many perils, as well as the fortitude of this mother under much suffering, was rewarded by a lenient sentence at the bar of the Old Bailey. Like the rest, she had sworn to suffer death rather than return to Botany Bay. But at the intercession of the renowned James Boswell, she was allowed to serve an additional six months and then to be set free.

Here was rich material for a piece of historical fiction with all the elements of adventure, romance, and voyaging in uncharted, savage seas. Little needed to be done except to fill in the backgrounds of the wedded convicts and to narrate their true vicissitudes in stirring style. But actually the authors added a great deal to the facts. The open-boat incidents occupy only six of the thirty-nine chapters. The book is taken up mainly with the youth of William Dew, the narrator, and the settlement and early years of the colony of which he was a part.

Reception of the novel was generally favorable through the years. A first review in the Sydney *Daily Telegraph* for June 6, 1896, reported: "Mr. Becke's intimate knowledge of the Australian coast has stood him in good stead in describing the voyage, while Mr. Jeffery brings to the partnership a thorough knowledge of the early history of the colony." The London *Daily Chronicle* said: "No maker of plots could work out a better story of its kind, nor balance it more neatly." The *Morning Post's* verdict was: "The novel is a happy blend of truth and fiction, with a purpose that will be appreciated by many readers; it has also the most exciting elements of the tale of adventure." More than half a century later, Dr. Colin Roderick termed *A First Fleet Family* "the first attempt to reconstruct the picture of life around Sydney Cove in the earliest days of settlement." [4]

The main defect of the novel lies perhaps in the choice of its teller, for the book is subtitled "a hitherto unpublished narrative of certain remarkable adventures compiled from the papers of Sergeant William Dew, of the Marines." No less a critic than Lord Rosebery privately remarked upon the implausibility of this character. In a letter to Becke written from Granada, Spain, on May 30, 1896, the noble lord averred concerning *A First Fleet Family:* "I could not lay it down till I had finished it," but added: "May I mention that I think Dew's marriage is a flaw? Up to quite the end of the story, we only realise Dew as a well-meaning bumpkin, and we suddenly find him marrying the beauty of the Isle of Wight and the daughter of a considerable landlord, at a time when sergeants were by no means so well thought of or classes so intermingled as now. I am not sufficiently conversant with the necessities of romance to judge whether this marriage was inevitable, but it seems to me extremely improbable. This, however, is only an incident and a minor incident in a graphic and interesting story."

A number of illustrations were made by R. C. Woodville for the serial version of *A First Fleet Family* in the *Illustrated London News,* some of which were not used. The amusing result was that Becke was assigned to write or adapt a story that might frugally employ these pictures. He wrote Jeffery from London on August 21, 1896: "Clement Shorter has seven drawings he could not use for *A First Fleet Family.*" Becke then proposed to rewrite a Becke-Jeffery story, "The Cruise of the *Policy,*" to fit the drawings. But he confessed on November 2: "Never again will I write a story around a picture unless it is a simple picture like the Crucifixion."

The second volume by Becke and Jeffery, written about the same time as the convict novel and published about a month later, reflected no great credit on either. This venture was a novelette, *The Mystery of the Laughlin Islands,* a rambling yarn which is mainly remarkable because of its rarity for collectors.[5] Its appearance as a separate volume was made possible only through the use of exasperatingly narrow page and line widths. Worth noting, though, is the fact that the site of the shore adventures is a group of out-of-the-way islands which are actually on the map but are still little known.

The third novel was *The Mutineer.* This highly appealing subject lay at hand in the libraries of Sydney—the most famous sea mutiny in history, the bloodless coup by which Captain William

Bligh's *Bounty* was seized on April 28, 1789, by a band of malcontents led by the Byronic chief officer, Fletcher Christian. This story, although known to the whole world today through the famed *Bounty* trilogy of Messrs. Nordhoff and Hall, as well as through two popular film treatments, had seldom been used in fiction when Jeffery and Becke talked over the idea and began the work that two years later resulted in the publication of their best book.

The yarn of the breadfruit voyage, the idyllic six months passed by the crew of the *Bounty* in Tahiti, the deposing of Bligh and his astounding 3600-mile voyage to Timor in an overladen open boat, the pursuit and capture of some of the mutineers, and the founding of the secret colony on lost Pitcairn Island by Christian's band and their Tahitian friends—all this is now so commonplace that it is hard to realize that when Jeffery set to work he did not have at hand the stack of *Bounty* documents since made available to scholars. However, he and Becke tried to make their version as authentic as possible, and in most parts *The Mutineer* sticks surprisingly close to the truth as far as we can ever know it.[6]

The first draft of *The Mutineer*, like that of *A First Fleet Family*, was mainly the work of Jeffery, but Becke, from early in 1896, worked hard to revise and improve it and to get it into book publication in the most dramatic form. And through the two years during which it was seldom off his mind, his faith in its high value did not waver. He wrote to Jeffery from Port Macquarie on March 18, 1896: "I really do think that this book will give us a great lift. It has, so to speak, got me by the 'innards' and I don't care what pains or trouble I take over it now, as I believe it will be both yours and my best work." On the 23rd he wrote: "Out of the three chapters you gave me of Part II, I am making four." In April he concluded, after attempting some revisions of chapters: "I am almost inclined to think that yours are the best after all," but he revised some quite heavily. More than a year later he wrote from London, on June 28, 1897: "I value this story more than any other work you and I have done." On July 1, when the novel was running serially, he worried that someone might steal the idea for the stage, and added: "I believe *The Mutineer* will make us."

An Australian publisher was the first to have faith in the manuscript, and *The Mutineer* was the first novel ever accepted by the firm of Angus & Robertson, although it was designed to be printed in London. The contract of June 6, 1896, which gave them all rights, paid Becke £75 immediately and another £50 on September 9. The first sum was added to the amount needed to get him to London with Nora and Miss Long. Soon after he arrived there in mid-August he wrote to Jeffery: "I hope to see *The Mutineer* dramatized, by the best dramatist in England."

III *"Hurrah for Tahiti!"*

The book, despite his efforts, was not made into a play, but finally a heavily cut version appeared serially in the summer of 1897 in *Lloyd's Weekly,* from which Angus & Robertson received £142. Book publication was held up by the slowness of A. P. Watt, who had been appointed agent for the Sydney publishers, and although Becke would not benefit personally, he was anxious that Angus & Robertson get their money back. He wrote on August 7, 1897: "A & R will do well to abandon their idea of publishing in Sydney. If Unwin takes it up they will get more money from him than they will by publishing it themselves. . . . If it is brought out *here* A & R may depend upon it being well noticed; if in Australia—dubious."

On October 21, in desperation, he wrote to suggest that Angus & Robertson should take the book away from the London agent. "Watt would not sell anything for £100 if he thought he could get £101 six months later. . . . I would forego all *my* interest in it rather than let it remain in Watt's hands until God knows when." But in a postscript he excitedly added: "Watt, I have just learned from Unwin, offered him *The Mutineer*. Terms £100 on publication on a/c of 25% royalties. . . . The price is not a good one, but it will anyway almost pay you (A & R) your £250 back."

Becke had tried hard to promote the acceptance of the manuscript, but at times was up against a clique of London critics and publishers' readers. An amusing example he reported on May 16, 1897: "Andrew Lang didna like *The Mutineers* when he read it for Longmans. But then Andrew Lang is notorious for condemning a story that has not—so I am told—something Scottish in it. We should have called Alexander Smith—the only virtuous man of the *Bounty's* crew—Dugald McWhannel; then all would have been well. . . . But for all that, Lang is a gentleman while his arch-fellow-worshipper of Stevenson—Edmund Gosse—is an atrocious snob of the deepest dye." Becke went on to mention a verbal duel with Gosse at a dinner party but promised to be more careful in future, because he didn't want *The Mutineer* to be "Gossed."

Disparities between history as we now guess at it and the plot of *The Mutineer* can be found. The task of Becke and Jeffery, however, was to tell an exciting story and not to write a history. Some of the differences may have resulted from incomplete research, but more likely they were made to add smoothness to a series of events which in themselves did not lack for natural excitement and climaxes.

The main character of *The Mutineer,* as he is in Lord Byron's poem "The Island," is Fletcher Christian. Becke and Jeffery properly open their novel on the beach of Matavai Bay at Tahiti, with a love scene between Christian and his brown-skinned sweetheart Mahina, who pleads with him in anguish not to leave the island. The second chapter shows Midshipman Edward Young pacing the deck of the *Bounty* and meditating on the love affair of his friend Christian and upon his own promise never to leave Mahina's cousin, the maiden Alrema.[7] Young is unaware until dawn breaks that Mahina has swum out to the ship and almost cut through the *Bounty's* cable, so that it would be wrecked on the reef and her lover could remain with her. When Young reports to the captain, he gets the expected violent reprimand that Bligh never spared any careless subordinate on his ships. Bligh's anger does not abate when he goes ashore to discover the guilty person, and in reply to Christian bursts out: "Beware, sir; you are treading on dangerous ground—you are mutinous! I've half a mind to make a prisoner of you and keep you under arrest until we reach England." Christian's anger prevents him from betraying his sweetheart to the captain of the king's ship, although as he says to her: "With us, who are servants of the King of Britain, no woman's love must count."

In the next chapter, "White Men and Brown Women," Mahina and Nuia, who loves Midshipman George Stewart, aid Alrema and other girls to steal the ship's cutter and help three of the crew escape to the hills. Young is put into leg irons for four days for allowing the deserters to flee, and the men are taken by Bligh and flogged for their effort. Before the *Bounty* departs—laden with a floating garden of breadfruit plants and bellying her topsails as she glides through the surrounding canoes and heads for the passage—Christian, on fire with indecision, replies to Young's entreaty to revolt: "If Bligh treats me as a man I will pocket his past insults and prove a cruel, heartless scoundrel to that poor girl. If he does not. . . ."

The bad blood rises in the next weeks as Christian is blamed by Bligh for attacks on the watering party at the Tongan island of Nomuka, and for the disappearance of coconuts from the deck. Christian's growing determination to escape from the ship reaches a crisis as the vessel nears the steep volcanic cone of Tofua, but on the evening of the 27th of April, he mentally crosses the Rubicon when a dozen chances conspire to enable him to take the ship without bloodshed. He discovers that "the way out" is to avenge the insults suffered from his tyrannous commander by returning to keep his promise to Mahina. The events of the actual mutiny are given in rapid-fire and authentic terms, the breadfruit plants are tossed in the ship's curving wake as the overladen launch containing the furious Bligh and his supporters heads out on its long passage, and the cry "Hurrah for Tahiti!" rises as the mutineers under Christian accomplish their grim purpose unhindered.

At once, however, Christian's leadership is not fully trusted. Midshipmen Stewart and Heywood have been held below against their wills so that two other navigators will be retained on the ship in case Christian is deposed. And the saturnine Edward Young has remained below to cast his lot with the rebels.

The first decision of Christian is to head for the island of Tubuai. There they will make a settlement and then go on to Tahiti and bring away their women to start a hidden colony, for should anyone on Bligh's launch survive by a miracle to notify the British authorities, Tahiti would be the first place visited by a pursuing warship.

On the way to Tubuai, an island south of Tahiti, Stewart and Heywood try to lead a counter-mutiny among those who wish to go directly to Tahiti, but their efforts are baffled by the alert Christian.[8] Attempts to land on Tubuai, however, are repulsed by well-armed and hostile Polynesians, and Christian in a council agrees to go to Tahiti before making a second attempt to settle at Tubuai.

Back at Tahiti, for six weeks the faithful Mahina has looked seaward and prayed to Oro that her lover Kirisiani might return to her. But her old mother has sought to induce the girl to forget her white sailor and marry the horrible Areoi priest Pipiri, who has sworn to take her within the month. He soon notifies her he has been told by a god that Christian will never return, and demands that the marriage feast take place the next morning. On the instant, Mahina descries a ship rounding the northern point of the bay, and gives him the lie. Then she runs toward the beach to greet her faithful Christian and the mutineers who have returned to claim their Tahitian belles.

IV *The True Tale of Christian's Death*

After a short stay at Tahiti and a native marriage ceremony which unites Christian and Mahina, the *Bounty* once more sails to Tubuai, with a complement of Tahitians and also, against Christian's wishes, the rebellious midshipmen Stewart and Heywood. A settlement is made ashore and a fort built which is strong enough to defend the newcomers when Pipiri, who had stowed away on the ship, leads the resident tribes in a fierce attack and is killed by a pistol shot fired by Mahina. Stewart and Heywood (as actually happened) again head a revolt and Christian agrees to return to Tahiti.

Part I ends with the third and final departure of the *Bounty* from Tahiti. A brief account is also given of the fates of those Englishmen who remain behind, either to die in the Society Islands or else to live and suffer capture by harsh Captain Edward Edwards of H.M.S. *Pandora,* imprisonment in irons inside "Pandora's box" (an iron-bound cage on her deck), and disaster when four of them are drowned in the wreck of the ship on a reef of Torres Strait. The sequel ends in England with the trial and eventual hanging of three of the mutineers from the yardarm of a warship.

The events of Part II, dealing with "the search for a resting-place" and the settlement of Pitcairn Island, give greater scope for drama and invention than the earlier part, which had to follow closely the known historical facts. Christian had made up his mind before leaving Tahiti that he would seek a refuge in the out-of-the-way island reported by Captain Philip Carteret in 1767 and named for his midshipman Pitcairn. The ancestors of Christian's wife Mahina were reputed to have come from an island called Afita, which Christian identifies with Pitcairn. By following the flight of homing birds, the *Bounty's* last crew—nine mutineers, along with two dozen Polynesian men and women—finally reach Pitcairn, their future home, which in truth had once been populated by Polynesians who had since mysteriously departed.

The superb description of Pitcairn Island in Chapter XVIII was probably written by Becke, who claimed in his "Autobiography" to have visited there and who had lived on similar high islands in the Pacific. The ship is driven ashore to her last resting-place, and when emptied of all that is useful, her hulk is burned and sunk in what is still known as Bounty Bay.

Trouble soon arises on this isolated paradise, however, when the proud people of Tahiti and Tubuai refuse to be degraded to mere hewers of wood and drawers of water for the arrogant sailors. Christian disarms Williams, who attacks Chief Tairoa with a knife, and in future times defends the native group to which he is allied by marriage. Mahina and Alrema (who has come as the consort of Edward Young) are alert to signs of trouble from the other white men, who are now free to give rein to their worst natures. Even Christian has allowed melancholy to overcome him as the depths of his remorse and exile become apparent. When his first child is born on a Thursday in October, he is so indifferent that he names the boy Thursday October Christian.

Unknown even to his wife, a roomy cave on the far side of the island has been prepared by him as a solitary retreat in which he would hide in case a ship of war penetrated the ocean wastes to capture him. He stocks it with food and ammunition, swearing to himself that he will never be taken alive.

Trouble breaks out again when the Tahitian wife of the brutal Williams falls from a cliff and is killed. Williams tries to take Nahi, the wife of Talalu, but the husband strangles the white man, blows out his brains with his own gun, and throws the body down to the beach. Thereafter peace cannot rest on Pitcairn.

Alrema in a song covertly warns the surviving white men of the killing. Christian emerges from his cave, tells them that Williams deserved his fate, and decides to take no part in the affair. At the request of Talalu, though, he gives a judgment, which is to submit to the white man's justice. Madly he then returns to his cave, and spurns his loving Mahina when she follows him. She then submits to be taken by Edward Young, who has deserted Alrema in a lustful desire for his friend's wife.

The five Polynesian men, aroused by Nahi, "mutiny" and kill Brown, Mills, and Martin. Young and Smith are spared, and Quintal and McCoy flee to the hills. But as Young says, "We must either kill or be killed," and led by Alrema, the white men take the brown men by surprise and kill them all. Nahi, in vengeance, leaps into the sea and drags Alrema to death beneath the waves with her.

Three years after the massacre, McCoy and Quintal discover how to brew a fiery liquor from the root of the ti shrub, and in a drunken frenzy Quintal throws himself headlong from the cliff. McCoy, equally aroused, tries to burn down the village and is shot by Young.

On the first day of the nineteenth century, a ship for the first time comes into view of the island. Christian, contrite and melancholy, seeks to launch the boat and give himself up to judgment. Smith wrestles to prevent him, and in the scuffle Christian falls with a bullet in his chest. In his dying moment he makes Mahina, Young, and Smith promise that he will be buried secretly, so that no other white man can ever point to his grave and say: "Here lies Fletcher Christian . . . mutineer."

Thus the novel attains a unity by focusing from first to last upon the character of Christian, to whom the fateful decision to overthrow Bligh was to mean the most in tragic terms. This tightness of plot was probably Jeffery's contribution and was little changed in Becke's revisions.

What really happened on Pitcairn will never be known, and Becke and Jeffery were entitled to use the bare bones of the story related by Alexander Smith, sole male survivor of the colony, when it was discovered in 1808 by a wandering American whale ship. Jeffery was undoubtedly aware of the three classic accounts, by Sir John Barrow, Lady Diana Belcher, and the Rev. T. B. Murray. And Becke claimed that they followed the native tradition on the various events.

His letter of June 17, 1898, to an unknown correspondent, which is found in the Mitchell Library, says in part: "We have not followed the printed records with docility. And I know the descendants of the *Bounty* mutineers and the *native* story of Christian and his life better than any man living. I have been told over and over again by *old* natives Christian was the very reverse of a sensual man; that he was intimate only with *one* Tahitian woman, whom he afterwards took away with him to Pitcairn; that this woman was seduced by his comrade Edward Young, but that Christian, horror-stricken at the bloodshed which had already taken place, actually protected the man who had seduced his wife; and the story of his life in the cave as narrated by Jeffery and myself is *true*—not embroidered fiction. Furthermore the story of Christian's death by a gunshot accidentally received from 'John Adams' (Alexander Smith) while the latter was endeavoring to prevent Christian from putting to sea in the *Bounty's* boat is, I believe, strictly true."

V *A Builder of Greater Britain*

The question arises, however, where Becke might have obtained a native version of the Pitcairn story that would be superior to the admittedly sparse report of Alexander Smith. Dr. Harry Shapiro in *The Heritage of the "Bounty"* writes (15) that there was almost a total lack of native tradition on the island: "I was told almost to the very phrases the accounts I had read for myself, and I discovered that these modern islanders learned their yarn not from some rich local tradition but from the very books I had myself consulted." However, Shapiro quotes as useful (34) a story handed down in the Quintal family proving that Christian decided to take the *Bounty* at the suggestion of Matthew Quintal. We must not discount the possibility that Becke might have met Tahitians to whom the whole story was a piece of their history. "Jenny," who gave several accounts later printed, escaped from Pitcairn in 1817 and returned to Tahiti to live out her life.

One contribution by Becke to *The Mutineer* was to make the Tahitian villain Pipiri a leader in the scandalous Areoi society.

Membership in such a group of libertines would be quite suitable for a Tahitian menace, even though the strange term "Areoi" required a footnote in the novel. From the time of Captain Cook, observers have noted this privileged band of priests, strolling players, and promiscuous child-murderers who worshipped the god Oro. In "The Areois,"[9] an article written by Becke at Port Macquarie while rewriting *The Mutineer,* he drew upon William Ellis's *Polynesian Researches* (1829-31), but also quoted the Jesuit Canova on a similar society in the Carolines: "It is absolutely impossible for the average human mind to conceive the frightful cruelty, the hideous debauchery, and unparalleled licentiousness to which these people surrender themselves when practising their soul-terrifying rites."

Becke wrote to Jeffery on March 7, 1896: "You will find that I will considerably alter that part concerning Mahena's lover. I am making him an Areoi (see accompanying ms. for T[own] & C[ountry]). This will considerably strengthen the story and bring out Mahena's devotion to Christian all the more strongly." Although nothing in his article or elsewhere suggests that homosexuality was a regular habit of the society, Jeffery must have had some doubts on this aspect, but Becke reassured him on March 25: "All your remarks *re* Areoism duly noted. We, of course, must avoid any allusion to Oscarianism, yet at the same time introducing the Areois into our tale will do good, I believe."

An even more interesting question than the historicity of *The Mutineer* is the fact that Charles Nordhoff and James Norman Hall were unaware of its existence, and had they known of it, probably would never have produced the three-volume account of the same events. Readers since 1932 would thus have been deprived of a fine trilogy, and a second film version would never have projected Trevor Howard and Marlon Brando upon the Ultra Panavision 70 screen without quite effacing the recollection of Charles Laughton and Clark Gable in the roles of Bligh and Christian.

A contemporary reviewer of *The Mutineer* felt in 1898 that Fletcher Christian and Pitcairn Island were already very old hat indeed. "While there is much to commend in the effort to revivify an old tragedy, it must be confessed that 'The Mutineer' is, as a whole, disappointing. . . . But, after all, the history of the mutiny and of Pitcairn is too well known, and is itself of too romantic a colour to give much scope to the novelist." [10]

Now, in the place where James Norman Hall comes closest to describing the genesis of the *Bounty* trilogy,[11] he mentions that he had picked up a copy of Barrow's book in Paris and had taken it with him to Tahiti. When one day he proposed to Nordhoff that they write the story of the mutiny, the reply was: "Someone must have written it long since." Hall answered that the only book he had seen was that by Barrow. Nordhoff was still unconvinced: "It's incredible that such a tale could have been waiting a century and a half for someone to see its possibilities." But after "the most painstaking researches," the only volume that the collaborators could find, aside from Bligh's own narrative and others by sea captains, was a children's book called *Aleck, the Last of the Mutineers, or the History of Pitcairn Island,* written in 1845.[12] Had they discovered that, two generations before, Becke and Jeffery had exploited the possibilities of the story and that a reviewer in 1898 considered *The Mutineer* to deal with a subject even then judged to be the essence of triteness, the Nordhoff-Hall team might well have turned their efforts to an entirely different setting than Tahiti, an open-boat voyage to Timor, and legendary Pitcairn Island.

The Mutineer finally appeared on June 6, 1898. In April, the Spanish-American War had broken out. On May 1, Admiral George Dewey had destroyed one Spanish fleet in the Philippines, and on June 3, Admiral Sampson had taken command of the blockade of another Spanish fleet bottled up in Cuba. The British publications were filled with war news and comment, and there was little room for book reviews. As Becke wrote on July 17: "One thing is certain; the book appeared at the very worst time any book could appear—the war news left no room for detailed criticisms on books and *The Mutineer* suffered, as scores of other books suffered, from that cause."

A special affliction rose with this particular volume. "About 4 days after it was announced, John Lane announced a book entitled *Mutineers,*" Becke wrote on June 21. "I wrote to Unwin on the subject. . . . What can I do?"

No American edition was copyrighted, and throughout the years *The Mutineer* has suffered from neglect. Justice to this masterpiece was finally done, however, in H. M. Green's monumental

History of Australian Literature (1961, 653-54), which comments: "The incidents are realistic and vivid, the white men and island women are as real as any in Becke's short stories, and they, especially Christian, develop as they must have done in the circumstances, and as Becke's [novel] characters do not. The scene in which Alrema tells the white men of the plot against them in her song; Talalu's appeal to Christian and his surrender; Christian's contemptuous reference to his little son; his gradual relapse into a solitary and brooding gloom: these incidents take us back to the northern epic; and, though their handling falls short of their desert, the book is a near-classic of Australian literature, and is likely to remain so unless or until the material is better handled."

Becke and Jeffery published two books on Australian history in 1899, with different firms. Each publisher was rushing to get his title out before the other, and Becke worried about the dangers of simultaneous issue. The first book came out in May, but the second was delayed until September. Two thousand copies had been bound with misspellings of the names of both the subject, Admiral Phillip, and the co-author, Jeffery, and were sent back to the printer.

The first of these books, *The Naval Pioneers of Australia,* was mainly the work of Jeffery. Becke had advised him: "The more gory and sensational it is, the better." In a generously illustrated volume the authors paid tribute to the fact that "four sea-captains in succession had charge of the penal settlement of New South Wales, and these four men, in laying the foundation of Australia, surmounted greater difficulties than have ever been encountered elsewhere in the history of British colonization." After chapters on the earliest Australian discoveries by the Portuguese, Spanish, and Dutch; a chapter on Dampier, the first Englishman to describe that continent; and one on Cook, the greatest of Pacific discoverers, the volume then deals with Governors Phillip, Hunter, King, and Bligh (who underwent a mutiny in New South Wales as well as on the high seas). Those daring young sea explorers, Matthew Flinders and George Bass, are also given their magnificent due. Becke, despite illness and other troubles, did some research in London and consulted with Emery Walker, who chose most of the illustrations. The book was very well received, especially because of the interest in Australian history aroused by the approaching federation of states in that country.

Both collaborators underwent great labor in producing the biography *Admiral Phillip,* which appeared in the series, "Builders of Greater Britain." Again Jeffery had done his research so well that Becke could find little to change, but he tried to contribute something from English sources. As he wrote Jeffery on June 8, 1897: "I shall put as much 'writing,' as you call it, as I can into the work but I quite realise that in such a book as this, *I cannot* improve upon your 'rendition' of the story. . . . I shall do my very best to obtain some information as to Phillip's career; but even the Admiralty have no records of it." Again, he wrote from Scotland on August 5: "I am now going through your 'Phillip.' It is very plain to me that you will have done all the work and that I shall have little to add. Therefore I shall not take half of the 60 guineas as I consider that that would be unfair."

VI *"I Can't Remember Anything"*

He wrote to the Earl of Pembroke, who read all the letters of his grandfather and great-grandfather (1767-1782) "without finding any mention of either Governor Phillip or of a Captain Herbert involved in the settlement."

Becke also made a fruitless visit to Bath, where the admiral who founded Australia had spent his latter years. The visit, however, elicited a letter from the Rev. Lancelot Fish, vicar of Bathampton, Somerset, and Becke rushed down to view the newly discovered grave of Phillip. A more speedy journalist anticipated him in announcing this discovery to the world, and Jeffery frowned on Becke's impulsive suggestion that the government in Sydney might be approached about putting up a monument to Phillip at Bathampton, because such an act might smack of publicity-seeking for their book.

Becke spent much time and money coming down from Eastbourne to London to consult with H. F. Wilson, editor of the series, and in trying to obtain information concerning the service of Phillip in the Portuguese Navy.[13] "To tell you the truth," Becke wrote to his collaborator on November 18, 1898, " 'Phillip' was a most disastrous affair for me, but I am not going to ask you to share the absolutely necessary expense to which I was put." The inquiries he started, however, resulted in a lengthy and valuable appendix based on documents in the National Archives in Lisbon.

This pioneer biography of the pioneer governor of Australia has been replaced by later fine works of scholarship such as that by George Mackaness, but is still worth reading. Wisely, since much information was lacking at that time on the full career of Phillip, the authors decided that their book should be "rather a narrative of the founding of New South Wales than a biography of the colony's first governor," and the tale of hardship and courage that follows fully justifies the prediction of Phillip to his superiors a few months after his arrival on the harsh shore of Sydney Cove that the settlement would prove "the most valuable acquisition Great Britain ever made."

Despite difficulties in revising and proofreading the contents when Jeffery was separated from London by thousands of miles of water, both authors were satisfied with the result. "The book so far as press notices go has been the success of the series," Becke wrote Jeffery in October, 1899. "Both Unwin and Watt said they had seldom seen such a simultaneous outburst of favorable reviews." Jeffery's opinion of their collaboration was expressed years later in an inscription in 1920 in a copy of *The Naval Pioneers of Australia* given to two ladies he had met on a sea trip.[14] After listing the joint works the co-author added: "Most of them are not worth remembering but Becke's South Sea stories were good and the life of Phillip and this book are quite good early history of Australia."

For several years Becke had been trying to find a publisher for a collection of stories and essays that he and Jeffery had written together from time to time. Such a mixed bag by two writers did not appeal to most firms. Moreover, the title story, "The Tapu of Banderah," had as one of its villains an American trader, and as Becke wrote to Jeffery on November 24, 1897, "There are some parts in 'The Tapu of Banderah' that the Yanks would not like." But Becke felt that the idea was a good one and persisted in seeking a publisher. "Certainly some of the joint matter was not good stuff," he admitted, "but the matter of my own which I have given them is some of the best I have ever written." He felt that Jeffery would approve of his efforts: "I am sure that you and I will be perfectly in harmony over the matter as we have always been." He finally found a publisher, C. Arthur Pearson, who put out the book in February, 1901.

This final volume in collaboration with Jeffery is difficult to assess.[15] The title story is typical adventure about a New Guinea island on which live an English missionary couple and three traders—English, American, and German. Arrival of a yacht bearing two English scoundrels and a chest of ill-gotten gold sovereigns starts a conspiracy between the traders and the captain of the yacht, an ex-blackbirder who had injured the people of Chief Banderah. The murder plans get out of control and a massacre results, but the British people are saved by the protecting *tapu,* or taboo, of the chief, and the English trader, to whom the reader's sympathies are closest, survives with his family. This novelette is neither the best nor the worst of the jointly written stories, and has a tighter plot than Becke alone usually contrived.

The stories by Becke alone have been mentioned in Chapter 3, and there is no need here to review the two sketches by Jeffery alone. Among the other collaborations, "Officer and Man" is a highly melodramatic tale of how a naval officer tried to protect from capture a good-hearted deserter who had once saved his life. "Foster's Letter of Marque" was the tale concerning the *Policy* which was rewritten in an attempt to fit Woodville's pictures; it was based on an actual sea fight between a Sydney whaler and a Dutch privateer mentioned in a previous sketch (64), and a rather strained story is superimposed in which the two captains are rivals in love. True stories of survival in the Pacific are retold in "Jack Renton" and "The South Seaman." The best piece in the book is perhaps "The Adventure of Elizabeth Morey," a New York young lady who in 1802 eloped with the captain of the American ship *Portland* and was one of the few survivors of an attack on the vessel at Tongatabu. After two years of suffering as a slave of the savage Tongans, she was able through tremendous bravery to warn the mate of another American whaler that its captain and boat's crew had all been killed ashore. She then leaped into the water and swam to safety as a battle began between the whalemen and the attacking canoes. The mate jumped overboard to help her, and later—for thus life imitates fiction—the pair were married. Following a suggestion by Becke that he keep an eye out for good material that might sell on the American market, Jeffery here came up with a true tale that should be better known, at least to all New York ladies who might be tempted to run away with a whaler.

Becke always freely acknowledged his indebtedness to Jeffery, and took great pains to make sure that his collaborator did not go unrecognized. A note written in Sydney on April 5, 1896, says: "This is scandalous and outrageous. Will be up to see you at once. I will cable him on the matter, and from this time my connection with him ceases." Apparently Unwin had advertised the forthcoming *A First Fleet Family* as having been written by Becke alone.

In an interview just before leaving for London, Becke was quoted as speaking very enthusiastically about his colleague's "possessing in a very great degree a faculty denied to himself, i.e., that of collating and drawing together the threads of a plot. Becke cheerfully and modestly admits that he himself is horribly lacking in consecutiveness." [16]

In London, Becke found the usual dislike of publishers for a double-barreled byline. He wrote from Deal on November 25, 1896: "Between ourselves, CKS [Clement Shorter] and others have (personally) objected to, in a friendly way, however, my collaborating; but I have I think overcome their objection by pointing to the success of *A First Fleet Family* and prognosticating a bigger success for A & R's book [*The Mutineer*]. I can assure you that *I* do not hide my collaborator's light under a bushel. In the proper time an illustrated article will appear in one of the reviews *re* L.B. & W.J." He was angry when Shorter's paper, the *Illustrated London News,* running *A First Fleet Family* as a serial, omitted Jeffery's name except in a "shabby italicized footnote at the end of the last chapter and said 'we are informed that this story was written in collaboration with Mr. Walter Jeffery.'" He was angry again when, reading proofs of *The Tapu of Banderah,* he found that Jeffery's name had been omitted from the title page. However, Becke himself forgot to add the name of the junior author to the article on Sir George Grey appearing in the *Fortnightly* for October, 1898.

For a man like Becke, who had as his main staple of literary material a recollection of a lifetime's activities, his confession of a bad memory to Jeffery on June 18, 1897, is amazing: "You know how terribly muddled I get with 'notes'—I have not your *wonderful memory* and although I can write *I cannot remember anything* and have to refer constantly to black and white." Other generous acknowledgments of Jeffery's contribution to their joint shelf of six volumes, as well as Jeffery's contentment with their efforts, testify that the relationship truly was one of happy symbiosis.

CHAPTER 5

Bully Hayes and His Supercargo

BECKE'S most famous creation was a real person—Captain William Henry Hayes, usually called "Bully," an American buccaneer who was the last of the great Pacific plunderers. Hayes was accused of swindling, ship-stealing, barefaced theft, bigamy, ravishing of young girls, murder, wholesale enslavement of natives—in fact, as Becke once wrote, of every crime in the book "except leprosy." He either eluded the warships of several nations or talked his way to freedom, and after thirty years of depravity he died of natural causes—that is, he was murdered on a stolen ship and thrown to the sharks by his cook, whom he had bullied once too often.

The amazing career of this South Sea rogue can be followed through documents which separate fairly well the truth from the mass of legends that have grown up about him.[1] Becke himself, as will be seen, added considerably to those legends, from first to last. His first lengthy writing, which did not even appear under his own name, dealt with a piratical figure not even thinly veiled under the name of "William Henry Hayston." And Becke's last, posthumous volume bore the title of *Bully Hayes, Buccaneer*.

The Hayes legend that terrified dwellers in that half of the world extending from the China Coast to the goldfields of Otago, New Zealand, was indeed horrifying. The truth of the man's life is in some ways even stranger.

I *Bully Becomes a Blackbirder*

Hayes was born in 1828, son of a Cleveland grogshop keeper. While yet a boy he stole $4,000 from his father and ran away to learn the sailor's trade on the stormy Great Lakes. He deserted his first wife before hurriedly leaving town on a stolen horse, and departed from the port of New York on March 4, 1853, as a passenger on the ship *Canton*. When the *Canton* arrived in Singapore in July, young Hayes had mysteriously become its captain, and a week later sold the ship for a good price. This was only the first of many episodes of barratry, for lack of papers or common justice never bothered Bully when a ship was there to be stolen. During his lifetime he treacherously decamped with at least a dozen of them.

He was successively and equally mysteriously master of such vessels as the American bark *Otranto*, the *C. W. Bradley, Junior* (this was the *Canton,* which he had bought back and named for the American consul at Singapore), the British ship *Orestes,* and the brig *Ellenita* of San Francisco, in which city Hayes deserted his second wife, Amelia Littleton, whom he had married at Fremantle, Australia. When the *Ellenita's* cargo of stolen beans shifted south of Hawaii and the vessel foundered, Bully and the crew made it to Samoa after four stormy days in a lifeboat. The Sydney newspapers reported his doings under the title of "The Career of a Remarkable Scoundrel," and for a while Bully was imprisoned in Australia for debt and then descended to acting with a troupe of blackface minstrels in the backblocks.

But his imposing figure—he was a muscular, bull-necked man with a dark mustache and beard, and the gentlemanly bearing of the born confidence man—soon enabled him to persuade a wealthy country landowner to finance the purchase of the bark *Launceston*. At Surabaja, Java, Bully sold the cargo of coal for his own pocket and soon slipped out of the harbor with a new cargo worth $100,000, owing £500 to his diddled agents ashore. He sold the *Launceston* and started a new stunt: selling tickets to passengers from Sydney to New Zealand in the ship *Cincinnati* and then sailing off without them.

While himself a passenger on the *Cincinnati,* he bigamously married again, a handsome widow named Roma Buckingham with five children. After touring New Zealand vaudeville houses with his actress wife, Bully showed up several months later as captain of the *Black Diamond,* appropriately loaded with coal out of Sydney. His expert seamanship was tested to the uttermost when a typhoon tore away the sails and he fought the storm for a fortnight across the tempestuous Tasman Sea. He sold the cargo, took on a new one, and slipped out of the harbor with all bills unpaid.

While the *Black Diamond* was hiding in a bay off New Zealand's South Island, Bully went for a sail with his wife, their thirteen-month-old baby girl, Roma's younger brother, and a maidservant. Caught in a squall, the yacht sank instantly, and only Hayes, who managed to swim ashore, was saved. Bully's growing list of enemies accused him of intentionally drowning his family, but nothing could be proved. Soon thereafter a whaleboat full of constables boarded the ship, seized the bereaved husband unawares, and took the *Black Diamond* to Nelson to be restored to its proper owner.

Hayes could always find another vessel and a woman when he needed one, and in the little coastal town of Akaroa he stole the tiny cutter *Wave,* aboard which he lured a sixteen-year-old Irish orphan named Helen Murray. When she would not yield to him and remained on deck even when gales washed great swells aboard, he "dragged her most violently, tore off her clothes, and eventually lifted her into a boat to take her ashore." There he talked his way clear of charges that he had abducted Helen and stolen the *Wave,* and soon talked another New Zealand lady into buying for him a schooner named the *Shamrock.*

Hayes disappeared from his haunts for a few months, and returned with a cargo of such curios as shells, imitation canoes, long-tipped spears, carved war clubs, and woven pandanus mats. He had become a South Sea trader. At the port of Lyttleton he married for the fourth time, to Emily Mary Butler, by whom he had twin daughters, Laurina Helen Jessie and Leonora Harriett Mary. Later a son Fred was born to the couple.

The paterfamilias sold the *Shamrock* and bought the sturdy brig *Rona,* which he mortgaged for £970—a sum which, of course, he never paid. The *Rona* did an excellent business, for this was the time of the Maori Wars that took so many fine lives on both sides, and Hayes smuggled gunpowder and lead to the bloodthirsty warriors at hidden coastal anchorages. To mislead official inspectors, Bully stowed the powder under the ship's cabin and littered the floor with straw. A single spark from a searcher's pipe would have blown the *Rona* to flinders, but Hayes made such a tidy profit that he was able to leave New Zealand for good.

His next exploit was to salvage the wrecked missionary ship *John Williams* from a reef on Savage Island, and for a price he carried the survivors to their posts on various Pacific isles. For a while nothing more was heard of him, and then in December, 1868, the *Rona* arrived at the sleepy town of Papeete, where its captain announced that he had 150 prime natives below hatches, for sale as contract plantation laborers. He summoned the sick, terrified, whimpering islanders on deck—Polynesian men and women who had been virtually kidnapped to serve a term of years sweating in the fields of their white masters. Bully was about to become the greatest of the Pacific "blackbirders."

"Oh, halcyon days of the sixties and seventies," Becke recalled later, "when the Pacific was not, as now, patrolled by men-of-war . . . ; when the Government agents, drunk nine days out of ten, did as much recruiting as the recruiters themselves, and drew —even as they may draw today—thumping bonuses from the planters *sub rosa!* . . . Merry times, indeed, had those who ran the labor vessels then in the trade, when Queensland rivalled the Hawaiian Islands in the exciting business of 'blackbirding,' and when Captain William Henry Hayes, of Cleveland, Ohio, U.S.A. —vulgarly called 'Bully' Hayes—came twice a year to fair Samoa with full cargoes of oil, copra, and brown-skinned kanakas, all obtained on the stalwart captain's peculiar time-payment system." [2]

The American Civil War had brought a new kind of slavery to the Pacific by making cotton growing profitable in northern Australia. Later, many more hands were needed for the Queensland sugar plantations. The demand for "kanakas" was great elsewhere, from Honolulu to Brisbane, from Tahiti to Fiji, and at one time there were more than fifty vessels in the dangerous "recruiting" trade. Among them were three operated by Hayes. Two were the *Rona* and the *Samoa,* both of which were lost at sea in 1869. The third was the most sinister vessel in South Sea history, the *Leonora.*

II *Boldrewood's* Modern Buccaneer

Originally named the *Water Lily,* built in Aberdeen for the Chinese opium traffic, she was renamed the *Pioneer* and put under the command of spade-bearded Captain Ben Pease, another American who was even more brutal than his friend Bully Hayes, whom he had met in the old China days. Bully's headquarters were now at Apia, Samoa, and at the time the *Pioneer* arrived in that port was out on parole under a charge of stealing men and women from Manihiki, where he had been marooned after the sinking of the *Rona*.

Hayes escaped to sea with his former pal Pease in the heavily armed brig, and returned to his old game of appropriating everything in sight, from coconut oil to native girls. A beautiful girl, actually, was the cause of a violent dispute between the two cronies, and one cruise later, when Pease and Hayes were dispatched by the German firm of Godeffroy & Son to the Line Islands for another cargo of blackbirds, something happened. The most likely story is that Pease was captured by a Spanish warship, from which he either jumped or was thrown while wearing full leg-irons which dragged him to a watery death. All that is certain is that Bully Hayes blandly returned to Apia, in full possession of the ship, which he now painted an innocent-looking white and rechristened *Leonora* in honor of one of his twin daughters.

It was on this evil ship that Louis Becke was to serve as supercargo, and this was the sort of man that he was destined to glamorize in his tales. Becke undoubtedly knew Hayes in his heyday. In many places he wrote not only of Hayes and the *Leonora,* but of the vile blackbird trade and the vengeance of kidnapped and mistreated brown cargoes.[3] And throughout his life, Becke's undisguised admiration for the rascally American produced a number of glowing factual and fictional accounts of buccaneering adventure.

Louis Becke knew and liked Americans. One of his earliest recollections at Port Macquarie was the arrival of five boats full of whalemen, survivors of the wreck on Smoky Cape of the *Adventurer* of Sag Harbor, New York. The lad was so anxious to greet them at the landing place that he fell down a cliff and lay for some hours with a sprained ankle and fractured arm. This mishap led to his first meeting with Captain Devine, master of the *Adventurer,* whom he later met on Fort Street in Honolulu.[4] Becke's works are sprinkled with characterizations of American skippers, missionaries, and beachcombers. It is significant that he first left his homeland for California, and in his semi-autobiographical *Ad-*

ventures of Louis Blake he describes voyages out of San Francisco. In a letter written to an American magazine less than a year before his death, Becke mentioned that he planned to cross the United States and revisit San Francisco, where as a boy he had met General William T. Sherman.[5] It was, of course, in San Francisco that Becke claimed to have first encountered the redoubtable Captain Hayes. The encounter in a Front Street saloon between the buccaneering Bully and the teen-age messenger boy who was to become his most energetic biographer and champion must have been only slightly less impressive than the first meeting of Dr. Johnson and James Boswell.

"When I first met Hayes I was a mere lad in San Francisco," Becke recalled in a not quite reliable memoir written during the last year of his life. "I had been in the service of the North Pacific Transportation Company." Dining in the waterfront saloon, Becke gazed at the famous alleged pirate and freebooter, and "saw a tremendously powerful man, with a heavy and carefully trimmed beard. He was dressed in white ducks, and wore a panama hat." When introduced, the lad noted that Hayes "had wonderfully bright blue eyes, that seemed full of fun and laughter." Hayes wound up by offering the boy a trader's berth on a good Pacific island, and asked "Can you fight?" Becke added that "five years later" he became Bully's supercargo.[6]

Elsewhere Becke wrote: "During the two years I was with Bully Hayes we visited many hundreds of islands."[7] In a letter published after Becke's death, he wrote: "I knew him when I was quite a boy, and sailed with him as supercargo and labor-recruiter for over four years."[8] Actually, as will be shown, Becke was on the roster of the brig *Leonora* for fifty-seven days, most of them spent ashore at one or another island. He associated with Hayes not for four years, but merely eight months, passing by far the greatest part of that time in a village to which he had fled from the wrath of the unpredictable buccaneer. But poor as was his memory, Louis Becke, as James A. Michener once said, was not a liar; he was a writer. And writing about Bully Hayes produced a number of highly memorable yarns.

Much has been made of the ironic fact that Becke's earliest writing about Hayes, and some of his best, was published in a volume bearing another man's name. Thomas A. Browne was a successful author who under the pseudonym of "Rolf Boldrewood" wrote *Robbery Under Arms* and a dozen other books. In 1894 he issued a novel called *A Modern Buccaneer*, without any acknowledgment that most of it had been written by Becke for a modest sum. Browne has been pictured as a literary raider much more piratical than Bully Hayes. The facts are not so simple as that.

Becke had been thinking in Sydney of collecting his stories to form a book. He asked and obtained some sound publishing advice from Browne, who in a letter from his home at Albury, on the border of New South Wales, wrote on October 3, 1893: "If you like to send me a description of a labour cargo cruise, pretty realistic—such as Hayes' when he delivered to Godeffroy's agent at Mille, I will pay ordering rates—about 20 slip will do—only send it at *once*."

Becke got busy "at once" and in less than a fortnight dashed off most of a narrative that takes up more than two hundred printed pages in *A Modern Buccaneer*, dealing with the hero's encounters with Captain "William Henry Hayston" and covering the wreck of the *Leonora* and the arrest of his young supercargo by officers of H.M.S. *Rosario*. On October 16 Browne acknowledged the manuscript and thought that with a little alteration it would fit in. He enclosed a check for the work.

Evidently Becke never saw any proofs. Browne wrote him on March 14, 1894, stating: "I don't think the 'Buccaneer' will be out before May." Becke had still not committed himself to the literary life, but was dreaming of joining the latest gold rush, for Browne added: "If you make up your mind to go to Coolgardie when the reefs are in work, which ought to be soon, I can give you an introduction."

When Becke first began reading a copy of *A Modern Buccaneer*, sent him by Browne, his interest "developed into profound astonishment." As he wrote Browne in part in a long letter of protest on August 6: "Of your book of 338 pages two-thirds consist almost solely of the M.S. I sold you. I notice that you have written from page 1 to the middle of page 8. From there, with the exception of part of the chapter entitled 'Poisoned Arrows,' my narrative proceeds with but rare and trivial alterations to page 224. . . . Of course, I sold and you bought and paid me for the

M.S. I was, as reference to our correspondence will show, satisfied with the transaction, although (at my suggestion) you gave me £12.10.0 down instead of the £25 you were to give me upon publication. . . . For additional M.S. I sent you from Manly you duly paid me and I certainly felt pleased that you deemed my descriptions, data etc. were of service to you; but I certainly did not imagine that this M.S. would go, without alteration, into your book as *your* work. It was a shock to me to find that instead of my material being used as a framework for 'A Modern Buccaneer,' to be clothed in your picturesque language, it was used *verb et lit*, and actually constitutes the book itself. *I* thought that under your skilful hands the story would be so changed and improved as to render my work entirely unrecognisable. . . . As for the monetary compensation I have received for the M.S., do you, as a man of the world, think that had I any conception that my story was to make, without alteration, two-thirds of your book, that even in my then necessitous circumstances I could have parted with it for such a very insignificant sum? The authorship of the South Sea part of the book is very freely commented upon by literary men and the marked resemblance of style to stories written by me has led to very direct questions being put to me."

III *"You Must Take a Native Wife"*

Becke's solicitor at this time was A. B. Paterson, affectionately known as "Banjo," author of many bush ballads such as Australia's unofficial anthem, "Waltzing Matilda." Through Paterson's mediation, Browne publicly admitted Becke's contribution in an advertisement in the Sydney *Daily Telegraph* of November 3, 1894, as well as in the one-volume edition that appeared in 1895. It is possible, however, that the premature exposure of the Bully Hayes story under the name of a more famous author harmed Becke's later income.[9]

The "Hayston" sections of *A Modern Buccaneer* are very close in details to other Becke accounts of adventures with Hayes, and although Browne presumably touched up the style here and there, this major portion of the book undoubtedly should be considered Becke's earliest and longest handling of Hayes in fiction. As Becke wrote Browne, from page 8 to page 224, with the probable exception of the Captain Kyte section of Chapter Eight, all the material may be found elsewhere covered in Becke's writings. In fact, to an extent unusual in a novel, a number of documents are included in Chapter Twelve concerning the naval proceedings against Hayes and the letters possessed by Becke, with names only slightly changed from what must have been originals from official files.

Hilary Telfer, the main character, a Sydneyside lad, in most of his adventures bears a close resemblance to Louis Becke. All the following incidents are biographical: a meeting with Hayes during the Samoan civil wars; the passage from Apia to Mili in the leaky ketch; the description of the brig *Leonora,* with name unchanged; voyaging among the Line Islands and the Carolines, and the presumed treachery of Hayes's partner Ben Pease; the visit to Kusaie; the wrecking of the *Leonora* in Utwe Harbor; and the subsequent riotous months on Kusaie. Especially good characterizations are those not only of Hayes himself but also of Lalia, the vigorous, handsome girl who helped to load the chests during the hurricane and who yearned to get back to her beloved birthplace on Easter Island. Particularly amusing are the portraits of King Togusa and Queen Sa of Kusaie, and of the "colored Chadband" Likiak Sa, the pompous native missionary sent out from Honolulu as assistant to the Congregationalist pastor. The terror of the hurricane and the suffering of Telfer after the wreck are told with dramatic immediacy. One may conclude, in short, that the best presentation of Bully Hayes in fiction by Louis Becke appeared in *A Modern Buccaneer* by Thomas A. Browne.[10]

Aside from *A Modern Buccaneer,* Becke produced little fiction dealing with Hayes.[11] He appears briefly and in a favorable light in a novel for boys, *Tom Wallis* (1900). In *The Strange Adventure of James Shervinton* (1902) Hayes enters several times. The protagonist meets him and turns down an offer of a trading post, feeling that: "I did not trust him well enough, despite his merry, laughing blue eyes, jovial voice and handsome face, for he was a man who could be all things to all men; and the blue eyes sometimes went black, and the smooth, shapely hand that was for ever stroking the long flowing beard liked too well to feel a trigger in the crook of its forefinger." (131) Shervinton reaches Ujilon just after Hayes's brig has departed, and finds on the reef a wrecked ship on which is posted Hayes's mendacious notice of possession.

More use of Hayes as a character is made in the semi-autobiographical novel *The Adventures of Louis Blake* (1909). The narrator dines with Hayes at Apia and breakfasts aboard the *Leonora,* but refuses a charter of his cutter to serve as a tender for that ill-famed blackbirder. Toward the end of the novel, in a complicated adventure at the dangerous Solomon Island of Buka, Hayes helps Blake and his men and in typical Bully fashion earns a profit at the same time. In the final chapter the teller of the tale comments: " 'Bully' Hayes and his doings—good and bad—seemed to be a never-ending subject of discussion, forming the framework for an extraordinary amount of fiction with most sailors, traders, and missionaries in the South Seas. . . . His was an extraordinary story indeed." (301)

It is surprising, therefore, that Hayes did not appear more often in Becke's fiction. Only two other stories have been found, and both might have a strong basis in fact. One is " 'Hope': A Memory of Bully Hayes," in *The Jalasco Brig* (1902). The setting is Kusaie during the period after the wreck of the *Leonora,* and the narrator, "the supercargo," is Becke himself. "Hope" is a ten-year-old orphan urchin (mentioned also in *A Modern Buccaneer*) who had been adopted by Hayes. He had been born on Hope Island or Arorae in the Kingsmill Group and was the only person who could soften that flinty heart. At the climax of the yarn, when Hayes's boat is overturned in the harbor at Utwe, the lad risks his life among the sharks to save the supercargo and Hayes. The portraits of both Hayes and the impish Polynesian lad are sympathetic.

A final story, only a few pages long, is often overlooked. "The Coward: A Sketch," appearing in *Bully Hayes, Buccaneer* (1913), bears the stamp of veracity. A trader at Koror Harbor in the Carolines, a Virginian who sports a brace of pistols at his belt but who is in all other ways unlike Owen Wister's cowboy creation, comes aboard the *Leonora* to report that his beautiful wife has been taken off by a young native chief and his band. "And what did *you* do?" asks Hayes. The answer is "Nothing. What could I do? There were twenty of them, all armed. I would have been shot down like a dog." Hayes asks if the man carries those pistols for ornament. "You damned miserable cur! You deserve to be shot like a dog! Could you not even put up a fight for your woman? You could have shot the flash young buck, anyway. Take off that belt." Hayes commandeers the unused pistols, orders his steward to pay the coward two twenty-dollar gold pieces, kicks him overside, and goes to breakfast.

Half a dozen other reminiscences of Hayes appear in Becke's bibliography, all recounted in Becke's most vivid and salty style. Naturally, the most authentic of these deal with the period of a few months during which Becke actually did sail as the buccaneer's supercargo on the *Leonora.* Putting together and collating the various memoirs, it is now possible to give a fairly reliable brief account of the great adventure experienced by the nineteen-year-old lad who dreamed of becoming a Pacific pirate, and lived to write about a real one.[12]

Young Louis, having delivered the worm-eaten ketch *E. A. Williams* to Hayes at Mili Atoll on January 17, 1874, and sworn never to set foot on her rotten deck again, signed on with Hayes as supercargo aboard the *Leonora.* This most notorious of blackbirding vessels was flush-decked, with sleek, yachtlike lines. She was armed with two guns on each side. All was shipshape, and the vessel was kept spotlessly white by a polyglot crew of thirty hard cases who at sea were kept in subordination by Bully's steel fist. But in return they were allowed two privileges unusual for sailors: they could buy as much hard liquor in the trade room as they could drink, and each one was allowed to carry along one native woman in the forecastle.

The trade room, which was to be Becke's domain, was kept like an ultra-neat country store, for into it Hayes would invite island chiefs and mulct them of their coconuts and turtle shell in return for brandy, rifles, fancy dress goods, and other amenities. The forehold was a horrible den in which as many as two hundred suffering "blackbirds" might be stowed at a time, and more than one of them was glad to end his misery by being pitched overboard into the deep Pacific swells. But the main cabin, in which the captain dwelt, was luxuriously fitted out with a notable collection of ancient and modern pistols and other arms, the former for ornament, the latter for instant use. From time to time, the cabin was the residence of one or more young native girls, with whom a cruise with the handsome captain was a thrilling change from the monotony of atoll existence.

A few minutes after Becke shipped in the *Leonora* he had a sample of Hayes's derring-do. Three tough men who had been beached by the captain of a New Bedford whaler came on board and asked Bully to sign them on. He refused in such "unnecessary" language that the leader of the gang offered to put a head on him. Hayes at once had the deck cleared and, taking the men in turn, knocked out each of them in one round. He then gave them a glass of grog apiece, and sent them ashore with a bottle of arnica to rub on their bruises.

Becke reported in his latter years in an unpublished manuscript that Hayes's favorite motto was a pious Spanish proverb: "*Estoy soltero; voy con Dios*"—"Although I go alone, I go with God." But Becke goes on to report:

"When I joined the brig in Milli Lagoon, in the Marshall Group, I was not surprised to find over thirty native women on board. Some of them were half-castes; and fourteen out of the number were the especial protégées of Hayes. He made no secret of the matter to Mrs. Hayes. 'As soon as I leave port I drop my conscience over the rail. I am a practical man, and do not want these women for myself. I make money out of them, and all the money I make is for my wife and children.

" 'Now,' said he, 'which of these fourteen girls do you fancy? . . .'

" 'I don't want any of them, captain.'

" 'But you *must* take one. If you don't you will be looked upon as a *moe-to-tolo* [a Samoan word meaning "the man who is too mean to keep a woman for himself but crawls into the bed of any sleeping girl"] and lose your mana and prestige.'

" 'I am no *moe-to-tolo*,' I remarked with a laugh, 'and I can assure you that I won't *totolo* to any of your women. Perhaps, later on, when we get to the Caroline Islands, and if I leave you as supercargo and go on shore as a trader, I'll take a native wife.'

" 'That you will *have* to do, if you want to gain the respect of the natives. And not one, but two or three, according to your mana.' " [13]

IV *The Wreck of the* Leonora

Heavy with arms, trade goods, and women, the *Leonora* prowled the southern Gilberts. Here, hoping to find coconuts, Hayes found a famine. He gave the natives food, and the first five who came on board ate so ravenously that they died. Then Bully took more than a hundred starving men aboard to transport them, at their request, to the German plantations on Ponape. Before leaving he gave the remaining population nearly a ton of rice and many casks of biscuits, saying: "You can pay me when the sky of brass has broken, the rain falls, and the land is fertile once more."

One March morning, after adventures in the Carolines, the crew of the *Leonora* sighted the high, verdant hills of Kusaie, favorite haven of all Pacific whalers. But they found that the island was being terrorized by five white men, who, aided by a gang of savage natives from the island ironically named "Pleasant," had domineered over the more gentle population and reduced Kusaie to a shambles.

This was the sort of situation in which Bully's brand of diplomacy could work miracles. After getting the approval of wizened old King Togusa, Hayes faced the five ruffians and demanded that they release all the Kusaie women they had stolen or the *Leonora*'s guns would blow them to bits. When the gang agreed, Bully charged the king a large fee, payable in coconuts, and as a gesture of comradeship offered to transport the whole horde of invaders to Eniwetok, where they could work for him collecting coconut oil.

But two nights later, as the overloaded *Leonora* sought shelter in a bay at Utwe to the south, a terrifying hurricane struck. Bully, with his vessel hemmed in beside the reef by two Yankee whalers, could not maneuver her in the gale. The last hours of the lovely, sinister ship are strikingly described by Becke in "The Wreck of the *Leonora*."

The trade wind lulled ominously, and the barometer dropped. Hayes had the royal and topgallant yards sent down, the boats slung inboard from the deck davits, and the wild Pleasant Islanders shut below, out of the way. Not a breath of wind was stirring, and some of them were so nearly suffocated that they got permission to swim ashore through the shark-infested waves. The brig was rolling so badly that the hundred extra souls aboard feared the *Leonora* would go over on her beam ends and stay there.

"The sky was black as pitch, and there was now a tremendous high sea, and the din and thunder of the surf on the reef a couple of cables' length away was most appalling. I had never heard anything like it before, nor have I since; and the weird sound of the huge seas as they tumbled and roared upon the hollow crust of the reef made my hair stand upon end like priming wires. The tide was low, and perhaps that had something to do with the wild, resounding clamor of the seas upon the long line of the reef; but there was a strange humming note underlying it all, which was new to many of our ship's company, and seemed to fill even the rest of the Pleasant Islanders who remained on board with a sense of dread, for they earnestly besought Hayes to let them come on deck, for, they said, 'the belly of the world was about to burst.'" (286–87)

Becke was just going to try to put in order his tumbled trade-room below when Hayes yelled for his officers to stand by. "From the northwest there came a peculiar droning, humming sound, mingled with a subdued crashing and roaring of the mountain forest, which lay about a quarter of a mile astern of us—the noise one hears when a mighty bush fire is raging in Australia, and a sudden gust of wind adds to its devastation—and then in another half a minute the brig spun round like a top to the fury of the first blast, and we were enveloped in a blinding shower of leaves, twigs and salty spray. She brought up to her anchors with a jerk that nearly threw everyone off his feet, and then in an incredibly short time the sea again began to rise, and the brig to plunge and take water in over the bows and waist—not heavy seas, but sheets of water nipped off by the force of the wind and falling on the decks in drenching showers." (228)

Boxed in by the whale ships, Hayes was unable to give the brig more than another ten fathoms of cable, because several deadly coral boulders were right aft. Bully Hayes's lovely vessel had only a short time to live.

"Seldom was a ship sent to destruction in such a short time as the *Leonora.* I had not been five minutes in the main cabin before a heavy sea came over the bows with a crash, carried away the for'ard deckhouse, which it swept overboard, killed four people, and poured into the cabin. I heard Hayes call out to the mate to give her another ten fathoms of cable, and then, assisted by half a dozen native women and a young Easter Island half-caste girl named Lalia, wife to one of the five white traders, began packing our arms and ammunition into two or three strong trade boxes. In another chest we stowed the ship's chronometers, Hayes's instruments, and all the charts upon which we could lay hands, together with about six thousand silver dollars in bags, the ship's books, and some silver plate. . . . We got the first box of arms safely up the companion, and Hayes saw it lowered into one of the traders' whaleboats, which was standing by under the stern. Then, as a tremendous crashing sea came over the waist, all the women but Lalia bolted and left us alone. Lalia laughed.

"'That's the long-boat gone, sir; and all those Pleasant Island women are drown, I hope—the damned savage beasts, I hate them.'

"I learnt afterwards that the crash was caused by the two guns on the starboard side taking a run to port, and carrying away the port ones with them over the side through the bulwarks." (289–90)

The same sea knocked the longboat overboard, but half a dozen Rotuma sailors leaped over and, using canoe paddles, saved her from the crunching coral. Becke was ordered to take charge of her, but before he could do so, a second comber fairly buried the ship. Becke and the Chinese carpenter, Ah So, saved themselves only by tangling in the falls of one of the quarter-boats.

The dismal drone of the gale rose again. Becke heard Hayes shout to the carpenter to stand by and cut away the masts, but it was now impossible to do so. The seas were sweeping the deck like a torrent. Soon the *Leonora* gave such a terrible roll to port that it seemed the end had come. Six big water tanks amidships had gone adrift.

During a five-minute lull, Hayes urged the remaining women to jump over and swim for the shore, as the brig's deck was now awash. "One woman—a stout, powerfully-built native of Ocean Island—whose infant child was lashed to her naked back with bands of coir cinnet, rushed up to the captain, and crying, '*Kapeni, ka maté a maté*'—('Captain, if I die, I die')—put her arms round his neck, rubbed noses with him, and leaped over the stern rail into the seething surf. She was found the next morning lying dead on a little beach, having bled to death from the wounds she had received from the jagged coral rocks, but the baby was alive, for with her dying hands the poor creature had placed it under a shelter, and covered it over with grass and leaves, where it was found, sleeping soundly, by a native sailor." (291)

There was now not the slightest hope of saving the ship, and Hayes coolly ordered the rest of the crew to get ashore as best they could. Becke and Lalia loaded another chest and, aided by Karta, one of the natives, was hauling it up the companion ladder "when the brig rose her stern high to a mountain sea, and then came down with a terrific crash on to a coral boulder, ripping her rudder from the stern post, and sending it clean through the deck." (292–93) The injured girl fell back in the cabin, but "one of the traders' whaleboats was lying close to, and the chest was, by the merest chance, dropped into her just as the brig came down again on the coral boulder with a thundering crash and smashed a big hole into her timbers under her starboard counter." (293)

"It's all up with her, boys!" shouted Bully, philosophically. "We must take care of the women."

Becke remembered that Lalia was still below, and with Karta and a Philippine sailor went to rescue her. She was sitting up in a bunk in the dimly lit cabin, her hair unloosed, her eyes shining with terror. Three feet of water sloshed about the cabin floor. "Just as we lifted the girl out, another sea came in over deck and nearly filled it; and with it came the bruised and battered dead body of a little native boy, who, crouching up under the shelter of the companion, had been killed by the wheel falling upon and crushing him when the rudder was carried away." (293–94)

Half drowned, the four struggled on deck and found the brig was quite under water forward, but the after part was hung up on the coral mushroom under it, rolled by every succeeding sea. Then a thumping wave swept all of them overboard. Becke and Karta got Lalia ashore in a mangrove swamp, but nothing was afterward seen of the Philippine sailor—except his right arm and shoulder; the rest of him had been taken by the sharks that infested Utwe Harbor. That terrible night, the sharks feasted.

V *The Murder of Captain Bully Hayes*

Hayes got ashore and at once began salvage operations among the castaways left on Kusaie. "And many a tragedy resulted, for

. . . mutiny, treachery, murder, and sudden death were the outcome of the wreck of the *Leonora*." (295)

The two whaleships had fled for fear that Hayes might capture them, and ashore a reign of terror began. The Pleasant Islanders continued their persecution of the bewildered Kusaie people under their feeble king. "One night, therefore," Becke later told a newspaperman, "our other South Sea islanders attacked these Pleasant Islanders with rifles, knives, stones, and bludgeons, and I went out under the idea that I could put a stop to the fray. They were all fighting like madmen, and I was promptly knocked down and a knife stuck in my head. It went right through the bone." [14]

Inaction bored Hayes almost to madness. He began to plunder the island as it had never been plundered before, and ordered young girls abducted to add to his growing harem. Suspecting treachery, he had some of his crew flogged until their backs were raw meat. One day he started out alone and declared war, unarmed, upon an entire village, driving the natives before him like sheep. Those were the days when an American missionary lamented: "Murdered men's bodies were picked up on the beach every morning . . . and the poor natives of Lele fled in terror of their lives."

One day, in a fit of rage at missing a trade ledger-book, Bully strode into the bedroom of the house he had built, driving out the women with savage oaths, and next moment reappeared with his arms full of chronometers. Standing in the doorway he tore the precious instruments from their cases and dashed them to pieces on the coral flagstones at his feet. Then, vowing that he would set a torch to the trading station he had erected and roast everyone in it, with his hands beating the air and his face grimacing with anger, he staggered like a drunken man to the beach and sat alone on a boulder.

This was too much for young Louis Becke. He boldly informed Hayes that he was going to leave him and dwell across the island in a native village. With a departing gift of a quart of gin from his remorseful skipper, Louis set out on the trail on the flank of Mount Crozier to the village of Leassé on Coquille Harbor. There for the remainder of his months on Kusaie, while the rest of the island reeked of mutiny and drunken violence, Becke spent an idyllic existence that afterward was to remain his most precious recollection of peace, and the subject of a number of warm sketches. "And the memories of the seven happy months he spent there remain with him still, though he has grown grizzled and respectable now and goes trading no more." [15]

Actually, the time passed at Leassé could not have been more than half a year, but such was the spell of his leisurely, dreamlike stay in the village with his native friends Kusis and Tulpé and little Kinie that several times in his tales he states that he was there for a year or more.

Then, as if the gods of the Pacific had determined to fulfill all the boy's dreams, the crisis came in the most dramatic way conceivable. A British warship, H.M.S. *Rosario,* steamed to Kusaie to bring Bully Hayes to justice, and Captain A. E. Dupuis, with a full complement of marines, formally arrested Louis Becke on a charge of piratically stealing the wormy ketch *E. A. Williams.*

Bully Hayes was also arrested, but few charges could be supported against him, for the big buccaneer was greatly feared by white and brown people alike, so that none dared to accuse him of criminal acts. Dupuis would have exceeded his instructions by taking off an American on such a charge as cruelty to native girls, who in those days had no rights whatever. It was doubly dangerous for a British warship to arrest a Yankee in 1875, when England had recently paid compensation of £300,000 to the United States for a breach of international law in the famous *Alabama* case. Hence the marines were amazingly careless about guarding Bully Hayes, and Dupuis was not at all sorry to hear that Bully had escaped from Kusaie on the night of September 27, steering a fourteen-foot boat saved from the wreck of the *Leonora,* in company only with another American, Harry Mulholland, who also had cause to fear justice.

This was the last that Louis Becke ever saw of his hero, but after standing trial in Brisbane and winning freedom through having retained, through all his adventures, a slip of paper giving him power of attorney for disposal of the *Williams,* Becke often thought of Hayes and followed his career and his legend. And when the time came for Becke to put to work his gift of words and his recollections of true adventure, Bully Hayes appeared in his pages again and again.

A disarming, two-fisted rogue, then, was Becke's most vivid

characterization throughout his writing years. Modeled on a real man with whom Becke had sailed and in whose service Becke had incurred a charge of piracy, this character from first to last was presented in various media ranging from newspaper interviews to lengthy sections of novels. Others besides Becke who knew "the real Bully Hayes" did not disagree too much with his estimate.[16]

Bully Hayes, Becke said in an early interview,[17] was "an extraordinary combination of bravery, vice, kind-heartedness, and savagery." His posthumous article on Hayes was probably his final commentary: "I have spoken of Hayes as I found him—a big, brave man; passionate and moody at times, but more often merry and talkative (he was an excellent *raconteur*); good-hearted and generous in one hour, hard and grasping in the next. He was as suave, as courteous and as clever as the trained diplomatist when occasion demanded the arts of civilization. He would 'haze' a malingerer unmercifully; but he never omitted a nod of approval or a word of praise to a sailor who did his work well. With women his manner was captivating, and no one entered more heartily into a romp with little native children, whom he allowed to do anything they liked with him." [18]

The exact details of the death of William Henry Hayes are not clear and probably never will be known. Nor do we know where Becke happened to be in that fatal year of 1877, but wherever he was, either in Australia or among the islands, he probably would have listened eagerly to any accounts of the death of his erstwhile skipper. In Becke's own final year of life, he wrote a version that appeared in an issue of an American magazine not nowadays readily available. For many reasons, it is worth summarizing here, as it gives a slightly different view of those events than the commonly accepted version of Charles Elson of Honolulu, who served as mate on the last vessel that Bully Hayes ever stole, or even the version earlier given by Becke himself in an interview.[19] Becke's final interpretation of the murder was a plot in which Elson was the guilty person. The motive was to obtain a sum of money that Bully had buried on Kusaie, the isle on which Becke and others of the *Leonora*'s crew had been castaways.

The final days began when the schooner *Lotus*, under Hayes's command, was sailing south of Hawaii: "Then he steered a south and west course for the Marshall and Caroline groups. All these details were given to the German authorities at Jaluit in the Marshall Islands by the man who murdered him, and were corroborated by the woman who shared his fortunes.

"I must now explain Hayes's object in running through the Marshalls and making for the Carolines, of which Strong's Island is on the eastern outlier. The day before he fled from the island in the small boat he concealed some thousands of dollars at a spot in the vicinity of South Harbor, and he was undoubtedly going there to recover the buried money when he met his death. It is quite possible that some day the money will be recovered. In all—having counted it, I know—there was nearly $8,000, not the $250,000 one writer on Hayes has written so glibly about.

"Of this $8,000, less than $300 consisted of good American and British gold and silver coins; the rest were Bolivian and Chilean half-dollars, worth but a little over half their face value. One bag of nearly 1,000 Mexican dollars Hayes took away with him to Guam. So much for the absurd story of $250,000 'buried in a cave on Strong's Island'—on which, by the way, there are no caves.

"After passing through the easterly chain of the Marshall Islands, dissensions arose between the mate and Hayes through the latter's refusing to put into Jaluit. The woman and his mate deliberately planned his murder. Coming up out of the cabin one day, after an angry altercation with the mate, the latter struck him senseless with the yacht's iron boom-crutch. He tumbled back into the cabin; then, still breathing, he was dragged up on deck and dropped overboard. The yacht then bore up for Jaluit.

"And this is the true story of the end of Bully Hayes. He was a much maligned man, and scores of writers who never saw him in their lives have made a good deal of money by their monstrous tales of his alleged murders, abductions, poisonings, and piracies." [20]

Such were the last words Louis Becke wrote about his Robin Hood of the Pacific, the big-hearted, big-fisted American buccaneer.

CHAPTER 6

A Mixed Cargo: Fiction and Non-Fiction

OVER the fifteen years of his active writing career, Becke supported himself and his family by meeting the needs of magazine and book publishers. He had early welded his typical style, but he taught himself, often painfully, to master various other forms than the brief narrative of South Sea adventure. Although always branded with the label of "author of *By Reef and Palm,*" Becke produced thirty-four other books (six with Jeffery) and countless uncollected short articles and book reviews.

Not all of these books were pot-boilers by any means, and had Becke soon returned, as he planned, to the life of a South Sea trader, literature in English would have lacked many a memorable volume. These other books should be remembered, because some of them contain stories that rank with his best work, as well as including a number of the non-fiction sketches or reminiscences that made him one of the foremost authorities on Pacific customs, fauna, and ethnology. A fairly large amount of his writing deals with his native country, and this contribution to Australian literature should not be overlooked. The present chapter will deal with Louis Becke as an author of novelettes, novels, non-fiction sketches with Pacific subjects, and works using Australian settings—works that do not come under other headings (for instance, quite large portions of his novelettes and novels deal with life in New South Wales and Queensland).

I *Cruises and Landfalls*

The novelette, in marked demand by magazine readers during Becke's literary career, was not a form especially congenial to his self-taught talent. Only in collaboration with Jeffery was he able to devise a unified plot that would run to more than a few thousand words, and the need to stretch the material often led to padding or to melodrama. For some reason, the novelette likewise brought out Becke's sentimental side, and he often cluttered it with sub-plot of a romantic sort.

His first novelette was published originally in Sydney in 1895, in London in 1896, and then (despite his fears that the Americans would not like it) in New York in 1897. *His Native Wife* does in fact offer an unfavorable, almost burlesque view of a New Bedford whaling captain and of the Reverend Hosea Parker, laborer for the "Boston Mission" in the vineyard of the Caroline Islands. The main character is young John Barrington, who has spent two years a-whaling in order to earn money to set up a trading station on Losap and rejoin his Micronesian sweetheart, Nadee. She has become persuaded by her scheming grandmother that "Jaki" has deserted her and agrees to give herself to Railik, son of the chief. Barrington is secretly admired by the lovely blond wife of the missionary, but he is faithful to Nadee; and even Helen Parker admits that, although in Europe or America a marriage with a native would be "shocking bad taste," in the South Seas it implies that "he meant to settle down and live decently."

When a landing boat overturns in the surf at Losap and the ship is blown away in a sudden storm, the climax comes in a rush. The conspiring Railik kills the missionary. Nadee, given a knife by her wicked grandmother to kill "the Christ-woman who stole thy lover from thee with her strong witchcraft," stabs Helen. A happier ending comes when José Herrera, a Bonin Island Portuguese who has been mate of the whale ship, elopes with Helen's sister.

This early experiment in the novelette was not followed in book form (except for the Jeffery collaboration, *The Mystery of the Laughlin Islands*) until 1901, when two stories of this length appeared under one cover—"Tessa" and "The Trader's Wife," a double offering quite favorably reviewed in the *Athenaeum* for August 17. The first of these tells of Harvey Carr, trader returning to the Carolines, who although convalescing from malaria is the best man on the hell-ship commanded by a scoundrelly captain dominated by a demon of a supercargo. When Harvey's sweetheart, Tessa, beautiful half-Portuguese daughter of his old boss, joins the vessel as a passenger, the supercargo plans to compromise her and force her into marriage, but a mutiny breaks out and a drunken fireman causes the vessel to burn to the waterline. Survivors take to three boats, and the captain and supercargo deliberately try to murder everyone else and almost succeed. The cast is reassembled on Pikirama or Greenwich Island, and it seems as if Harvey's dying moment has come; but just in time a Savage Islander seeking *utu* or revenge executes justice. All in all, this novelette describes a trip that might dismay even a girl like Tessa, who always carries a Smith and Wesson revolver in her blouse. The whole tale could have been told in much less space and the plot contrived in fifteen minutes.

"The Trader's Wife," somewhat shorter, takes fifty pages of maneuvering to tell how a faithless woman and her paramour, who had once written her that life would be "happiness unutterable, even in a desert place," were marooned by her sea-captain husband on desolate, volcanic Hunter's Island.

"Yorke the Adventurer," in the volume of that name (1901), is one of the best of Becke's novelettes, and the title character one of his finest creations. "Yorke" is discovered on the south side of the cannibal island of New Britain, alone on his cutter, which not long since had been attacked and whose crew had all been massacred. Ashore at the time, he had boldly recaptured the vessel and single-handed sailed it to this isolated cove. When he needed to sleep, he kept the black warriors at a distance by sprinkling shards of broken bottle-glass all around the deck.

Tom Drake, supercargo of the *Fray Bentos,* and Captain Guest invite Captain Yorke, whom they admire for his courage and seamanship, to sail in company with them. Yorke's skill is fully tested when he and Drake are marooned on an islet during a hurricane and succeed in rejoining the ship after a battle between canoe-loads of native killers and the two white men, who paddle out on a raft. The secret of Yorke's past—he killed his wife's lover in a duel and deserted from the German Navy—is revealed before his rather sudden death. The sequences are thrilling but not unconvincing, and the conclusion shows that life can be grim for at least some people who seek refuge in the Pacific. "But here, Guest, and you, Drake . . . your hands. I'll be dead by tomorrow morning . . . and wish good luck to you both, before I begin babbling silly twaddle about things that are of no account now. But the South Seas are a rotten sort of place, anyway." If Louis

Becke ever met in all his wanderings a man half so powerful and noble as the Yorke he portrays, his skill in realistic characterization is here well demonstrated.

The next novelette, also used for a book title, was "The Strange Adventure of James Shervinton" (1902). Although this story is still worth reading, the form again betrays Becke and interest flags. The hero, of high British blood, after fifteen years of wandering in the Pacific is stuck as a trader on the Gilbertese isle of Tarawa, a name well known to certain United States Marines. Jimmy or "Simi" Sherry, as he is called, has a strong desire to rival some of the high feats of earlier adventures in the South Seas, and his chance comes when Niabon, the "witch girl," contrives that he make a long voyage with her and other natives, as well as the beauteous widow of Krause, a German trader (her husband was a brute who had just been murdered by the Gilbertese people in order to protect their friend Simi). Shervinton succeeds, despite many encounters, in bringing the small sailboat over stormy seas for 3200 miles, all the way to Lucia Krause's home island of Guam. Torn between the charms of Niabon and Lucia, he feels most drawn to Niabon but proposes marriage to the widow. The dilemma solves itself by tragedy. The day they arrive, everyone goes ashore on Guam except Shervinton and one faithful crewman. The brave boat is driven to destruction by a tidal wave, and the hero regains consciousness two weeks later, to learn that Lucia and Niabon, along with three hundred others, had perished in a great earthquake.

The odyssey of the small boat, by which Shervinton does indeed achieve a triumph of navigation, has its moments—especially during the episode in the lagoon of Apemama, where a gang of King Apinoka's men almost capture the fugitives and their weapons in a bloody stern chase. The best part of this longer story, written when Becke was mature in his craft, is its background of native life and especially the portrait of Niabon, mysterious and alluring. Even without her famed power of prophecy she can predict what will befall the "man with the strong will to accomplish all that is before him," and can face generously the truth that she can have no share in this man's destiny. The touch of supernaturalism adds to what would otherwise be one more adventure story.

Little need be said about another novelette, "The *Jalasco* Brig" (1902). Like the novel *Edward Barry,* it deals with the recapture of a trading vessel taken by pirates.

Becke did better when he returned to his native Australia for material for another long story. "Chinkie's Flat" (1904) is a novelette about a young man who buys a broken-down crusher in the abandoned gold camp of the title, and by good sense is able to harmonize the interests of a few remaining miners and a band of wandering Chinese who are willing to hire out as laborers to reclaim the rich tailings. The reader gets interested in the mining story but suddenly is switched to Townsville, where, to supply romance that later results in three weddings, a heroine arrives who is to be governess at a distant inland cattle station. The high point of the story is the scene when Grainger is escorting Sheila Carolan through a region that is the range of wild blacks led by two savage ex-policemen, and she is captured when left alone during a storm. But all problems are solved by a few unerring rifle bullets, and no character is really vivid except a horrible woman who keeps a boarding-house in Townsville.

Often overlooked is another novelette, "John Frewen, South Sea Whaler," in *Chinkie's Flat.* The main figure is one of the six sons of a New Hampshire farmer, who at the age of twenty-five becomes a navigator and second mate of the *Casilda.* Because he objects to the hazing of a half-Samoan boatsteerer, he and his friend desert, sacrificing their "lay" on the profits of the voyage, and find friends on the island of Manono when they help to recapture the fine ship *Esmeralda* from mutineers. Mrs. Marston, young wife of the murdered captain of that ship, is kidnapped by the crazed Italian ex-mate while Frewen, the new captain of the *Esmeralda,* is away on a trading voyage.

The unity of this longer story is fairly well maintained, and the love interest is not too sickly, for Amy Marston is a brave woman and mother, able to survive a month of drifting on a murder ship and seven months on a lost atoll until the searchers led by the devoted Frewen are able to come to the rescue. A minor figure, who gives Frewen advice on a labor-recruiting voyage which does not come to pass, is a Sydney merchant named Beilby, and we are reminded that Becke's mother's father was a Sydney merchant named Beilby. "Uncle Beilby" also appears in a novel, *The Adventures of Louis Blake.*

No novelette appeared in Becke's books for four years (except for "The Settlers of Karossa Creek" in a 1907 volume written for young people). The last of Becke's novelettes appeared in *The Pearl Divers of Roncador Reef* (1908). The title story, although suggesting much that could be done with a setting among the seekers of mother-of-pearl shell in a hidden Solomon Island lagoon, is disappointing and routine. Three fine men, down on their luck in Townsville, a spot north of Capricorn, become partners to seek this lagoon, and on the way, after stormy weather, at Mboli Harbor rescue Edith Chesson, daughter of a murdered trader. With better luck filling their sails, they reach Roncador Reef, "the Snorer," off Palan Island, and the lady sets up a trading store not far away. One of the partners, Sedley, with an injured foot, goes there to recover, and saves Edith from the villainous Clissold, who has pursued her all the way from Mboli in time to supply a menacing finale. Dr. Carew, noble protector of Edith who is silently in love with her, gives the younger couple his blessing. The ship returns filled with shell; everybody is rich and, to use a frequent Beckean phrase, happy as sand-boys. This sort of story boiled the family pot, but Becke's reputation ran no risk when he decided not to print any more novelettes.

The full-length novel, although it offered some of the same dangers as the novelette, offered more scope as well. Uneven in craftsmanship here as elsewhere, Louis Becke could be both at his worst and his best when it came to tackling the novel.

II *Voyaging in Perilous Seas*

Becke wrote on his own, in addition to his work with Jeffery, seven volumes of full-length fiction. Admittedly, he was not comfortable in the longer form, and his work is often pseudo-biographical or is a string of episodes without a unified plot, in which a red-blooded young Britisher, motivated by luck or casual encounters, wins through against odds and gets a fortune and a sweetheart in the end. A surprising amount of background material for his novels is drawn from his Australian experiences in Sydney, northern New South Wales, and Queensland.

His first long story was the "boys' book" that he proudly wrote to Jeffery that he had sold to the Religious Tract Society. Entitled *Tom Wallis, a Tale of the South Seas,* it is better than the average Sunday school reading matter of 1900, and full of lively Pacific adventure; Captain Bully Hayes appears as a minor and far from menacing character. The moral tone of the publisher and the mild language of the book caused one reviewer to label Becke "the pirate turned Puritan!"

In the same year followed a short novel, *Edward Barry, South Sea Pearler.* The hero, age thirty, departs from Sydney with only three shillings in his pocket, as mate of the brig *Mahina,* a murder ship bound to a secret lagoon on the island variously named Arrecifos, Providence, or Ujelang, in the western Marshalls, which Becke had visited in company with Bully Hayes, one of whose richest stations it was. Here Barry discovers Alice Tracey, wife of the murdered owner of the brig, and after the vessel is loaded with valuable gold-lipped shell, he deftly manages to turn the tables on all the blackguards aboard and sail back to Sydney with a cargo worth £40,000 in shell and pearls. The girl he left behind had conveniently married another man, and Edward is free to reveal his devotion to the rich widow. The yarn is machine-made and seems interminable, and even the technique of pearl-diving, about which Becke knew a good deal, is skimmed over in favor of campfire chats with Alice, the lovely castaway. The reviewer in the London *Daily Times* for August 6, 1900, called this novel the best thing Becke had done. But on September 15, a jeering London paragraph writer remarked that since *Chambers's Journal,* in which the story appeared serially under the title of "Arrecifos," was notoriously a moral publication, "no dramatic intrigues of white men and brown women can find place in its columns. Becke has to confine himself to thin sentiment—and blood."

Becke's next novel, however, is one of his very best, and does not deserve the oblivion it has suffered. *Breachley, Black Sheep* (1902) moves along steadily and shows a maturity in emotional portrayal combined with a use of Becke's richest veins of reminiscence. William Breachley much resembles Louis Becke in his early years, and is not a very black sheep, for his motives are usually innocent and decent. His boyhood days correspond to those of young Becke, although the father in the novel is a lumberman or "timber-getter" who wants all his sons to help him in the sawmill.

Young Billy at the age of thirteen becomes a criminal when he and the red-haired niece of the brutal Scotch schoolmaster decide to get revenge on him when the man is lying drunk, trying to consume his semi-annual keg of rum. To destroy the liquor, the children put the keg on the fire. The ensuing explosion burns down the schoolhouse and singes the master's beard, and Billy and Mary flee down the shore to take shelter with a friendly smuggler. A meal of poisonous shellfish results in the capture of the sick arsonists by Sergeant Finnegan.

Early scenes on the coasts of New South Wales and of Queensland, where Breachley is sent with a party to cut cedar logs in cannibal country, are followed by chapters concerning his involvement with a devil-may-care friend named Harry Brandon, who has all the manly virtues but also has a fiery temper and is a lion among ladies. When the young men are in Sydney, and Brandon is having an affair at a Botany Bay hotel with the wife of a French general, the two get into a fight and Breachley is put in a hospital for a week, but his friend is temporarily cured of philandering.

The scene changes when Breachley is shanghai'd at Newcastle and begins a series of wanderings in San Francisco and the South Seas—part of the time in company with his brother Morgan. Dutifully, William gets into a scrape in the Paumotu Group by running off with the beautiful half-English native wife of a French schooner captain. Their sailboat piles up on Tahanea and poor Hino is killed in the surf. Breachley wanders as a whaleman, trader, and blackbirder, but finally returns to the fold of respectability, and the fates of all the characters are neatly wrapped up at the end.

The characters of Brandon and of Billy's Aunt Selina in Sydney are strongly drawn, and there is enough of the impetuous but decent instincts of Breachley to make his story worth following to the finale. Some scenes—especially the existence of the Queensland timbermen and, curiously, waterfront life in San Francisco around 1870—are among Becke's best. All in all, this novel could be recommended to those who feel that Louis Becke never could turn out a long story comparable to those being published in English during his writing years.

Helen Adair (1903) was composed partly in Ireland and partly on a voyage to Jamaica and the United States, but it is a semi-historical novel of the convict days in Australia. Helen is a lovely and loyal colleen who, when her father and cousin are transported for publishing political pamphlets, deliberately passes counterfeit money so that she also will be sent to the penal colony. The three relatives are widely separated, but her cousin escapes from Van Diemen's Land and becomes a bushranger near Waringa Creek in New South Wales, where Helen is handmaid to the wife of Colonel Lathom, head of the convict settlement. A fine young American named Lugard, acting for a society devoted to rescuing such political victims, requires many months to get in touch with all three and put them aboard the American whaler *Palmyra.*

They sail from Sydney, but soon Helen's father dies and is buried on the coast. Then they head for Batavia and freedom, but the ship, helped by a friendly Dutch vessel, the *Leeuwarden,* has to fight off a pursuing gunboat. Then, in the night, both ships run aground on Wreck Reef, where Matthew Flinders the explorer spent some despairing days in 1803. Most of the people in the *Leeuwarden* are transferred safely to the *Palmyra,* which has been tossed over the reef into the safety of the lagoon. One survivor is a lady, Helen's former mistress, who had eloped with Lieutenant Wray. Wray decides to stay with the sinking *Leeuwarden* and is killed, and his despairing sweetheart jumps overboard as the *Palmyra* once more heads for the open sea.

This novel is so good that one wishes it could have been better, for the material is not trite and the plot is fairly well woven. Passages inveigh against the evils of the old convict "System," and one villainous character, the Rev. Joseph Marsbin, is undoubtedly a caricature of the historical figure of Samuel Marsden, who as principal chaplain of New South Wales made money from raising sheep but was such a bitter enemy of the "emancipists" that he resigned from the magistrates' bench rather than sit with two convicts who had served their time; Marsden was labeled by Governor Macquarie as "a malevolent man clothed in the garb of humanity and hypocritical religious cant." Becke was also aware of the amazing escape from West Australia of John Boyle O'Reilly, who at the age of twenty-three got away to Boston and became an American author and leader in helping Irish friends to escape from Australia (O'Reilly's *Moondyne,* Boston, 1879, is the best of the early novels about Australian convictism). The setting of Becke's novel is quite authentic and most of the actions are convincing, but Helen herself is so patient and sweet under suffering that the reader cannot swallow such a dose of virtue. Helen's choice for marriage at the end, surprisingly, is neither her boyhood sweetheart and cousin nor the noble American Lugard. No worse than the average conventional English novel of the early part of our century, *Helen Adair* fails because it is too conventional and, despite some fighting and escape scenes, too saccharine for most tastes today.

Tom Gerrard (1904) has as setting the cattle stations and gold-mining camps of Northern Queensland, and furnishes information on these occupations, which Becke followed during his wandering years. But the story is mechanical and easily predictable. Gerrard owns Ocho Rios, northernmost station on Cape York Peninsula. He loves Kate Fraser, daughter of a Scottish miner, who is also pursued by a fine young parson and by Randolph Aulain, formerly an officer in the hated Black Police but now a gold-hunter. Tom buys Kaburie Station near Fraser's Gully and rescues Kate from an alligator. A big bank failure ruins Tom and all his friends financially, and Ocho Rios is almost destroyed by a bush fire. Later, in order to recoup his fortunes, Tom takes his step-sister and her two young wards to settle at Ocho Rios, and Kate, living nearby with her father, advances the romance by rejecting Aulain. Tom then is accepted, but before the wedding, the madly jealous Aulain strikes him with a whip and then commits suicide. And a rousing finish is supplied when Tom and his aboriginal "boy" Tommy are attacked in the night at Rocky Waterholes, and, although both are wounded, wipe out four members of an evil gang that had robbed the safe on the coastwise steamer *Cambier*. Despite the authenticity of the book's settings, the tone is tired, and not even the main character comes to life in its pages.

The Adventures of a Supercargo (1906) adds little to Becke's repute as a novelist, even though its hero is Tom Denison, his *alter ego* in many a good shorter piece. Tom at this time is only sixteen years old, however, and there is nothing in the story that could not be enjoyed by a twelve-year-old who likes to read of South Sea derring-do. Tom, an orphan reared by an unlovable aunt, is caught in a storm in his sailboat beyond Sydney Heads and is picked up, boat and all, by a well-intentioned gang of pirates who by stealing a ship are getting a deserved revenge on the owner. Tom is forced to sail with them to Rapa and Easter Island, but there shifts over to serve as supercargo on a vessel bound for Samoa. Here its captain takes a charter from an American named Ross to go pearl-shelling among the cannibals of Admiralty Island. Outwitting an enemy gang led by the escaped convict who had killed Tom's father, the traders not only win a load of valuable shell but also a fortune in salvage from a derelict brigantine loaded with trade goods. Tom returns home, a seasoned supercargo, to his beloved little sister, and henceforth even Aunt Christina must admit that he is now a man.

Becke redeemed himself, however, in his last novel. In many ways, *The Adventures of Louis Blake* (1909) is his best, if one wants a rattling account of what a young man of energy and alertness might accomplish in the wide Pacific before the days of steam. This is Becke at his most autobiographical, and as if to underline its factuality he has changed the name of his narrator by only two letters from his own.

The story opens in 1870 in San Francisco, where young Becke was really a messenger boy, and he is accompanied by two older brothers, Vern and Alf, who were drawn from actual brothers. Louis's "Uncle Beilby" is mentioned as having recommended that he and Vern join Alf in California and arranged for their voyage on the *Lily of France* with a mean-minded captain. But the rest of the tale does not jibe with what we can tell about actual adventures of Louis Becke—not Blake—in these early years. The lad, losing his position in the bookshop of A. L. Bancroft & Company in Market Street because he spends some time reading the books, finds that his brothers have also lost their places and they must separate.

Blake gets a place helping the purser of a supply vessel for a colonization scheme on the coast of Lower California, but the ship is captured by mutineers and Louis signs on with the Yankee whaler *Pocahontas*. After some episodes reminiscent of *Moby*

Dick, which might have furnished some background (Becke wrote a glowing introduction to a 1901 edition of Melville's novel), the reader is given further exciting incidents of Cocos Island treasure-hunting and of South Sea trading, fighting and gun-running in the Samoan civil war, and blackbirding in the Solomons. After each encounter, Louis Blake's luck or pluck brings him advancement that eventually makes him a successful trader in the Carolines and leads to his reunion with his wandering brothers. As mentioned in Chapter Five, Bully Hayes appears in this last novel in his typical role.

The only woman character in *The Adventures of Louis Blake* is an old Irish landlady in San Francisco, although the narrator claims to have witnessed the celebrated shooting by Laura D. Fair of Judge Crittenden on the steam ferry *El Capitan*, an event that changed California history. Altogether, one might conclude that, of all the novels, this is the best to choose if a fast-moving yarn of Pacific enterprise is sought. Amusing is the comment made three generations ago, when Blake thus describes Tahiti: "One of the loveliest places in the South Seas, and not then, as it is now, over-run by globe-trotters, tourists, and blatant commercial travellers from Yankee-land." (239)

III Wild Life in Southern Seas

Early in his writing career, Louis Becke was hailed as one of the admirable tribe of amateur naturalists, and it is true that much of his writing concerns his personal knowledge of the fauna and flora of the Southern Hemisphere. Many of these sketches are fascinating first-hand accounts of strange animals and sea denizens. Becke's favorite sports were fowling and fishing—especially fishing, for anything from lowly leatherjackets to mighty whales. Advice to anglers is found scattered through many of his books.

His first volume of non-fiction was titled *Wild Life in Southern Seas* (1897) and well demonstrates his qualifications for his fellowship in the Royal Geographical Society. The *Spectator* for December 15, 1897, called this volume a tribute to "a knowledge begotten of long personal acquaintance and coupled with the ability to write good nervous English" and termed its author "a keen and most competent observer as well as a *raconteur* of the first excellence." The reviewer in *Literary World* for January 7, 1898, said that it "shows Mr. Becke at his best. There is much less of murder and outrage and more of the humanities and of Nature in her varied moods in the volume than in its predecessors."

Wild Life is still well worth reading. Perhaps the best pieces in it are "The Areois," already mentioned in connection with the novel *The Mutineer;* "Jack in the Atolls," a discussion of the shark-catching business; "Deep-Sea Fishing in Polynesia," set mainly off Nanumanga and the reef of the Tia Kau; and "The Old and the New Style of South Sea Trader"—a topic on which Becke, former trader, had much factual information to convey.

Three more good sketches are to be found in *Rídan the Devil* (1899). "In a Native Village" tells of how a new trader was saddled with the misdeeds of a horse left by his predecessor, and how the native people hoped that by fining the newcomer heavily, they would be able to outshine the church of a rival village: "People say that when you pay that horse's fine they will buy pine windows, pine doors, and pine floor, *and give Halamua church hell.*" A horrifying picture is given in "Bobaran" of a trader's life on the cannibal island of New Britain. The volume ends with "A Christmas Eve in the Far South Seas," set on the Marshall island of Mili. It is a rather nostalgic recollection of a holiday beside a lagoon under the Equator, celebrated by two British traders, two Americans, and two Germans, who try to forget their national rivalries for a day devoted to peace and the consumption of rum, as well as a giant cake. They even make an effort to concoct a Scottish haggis; of it the narrator's boat's crew said that "it *smelt* good, like shark's liver, but was not at all so juicy."

Three sketches in *By Rock and Pool* (1901) are also interesting. Two of them deal with angling adventures: "The Fisher Folk of Nukufetau" and "Jack Shark's Pilot," the latter mentioning the superstition at Futuna that killing a pilot-fish brings bad luck. The concluding one is entitled "A Cruise in the South Seas: Hints to Intending Travelers." It is mainly a reminiscence of Becke's various journeys around Samoa, but many of his seasoned remarks, although written around the turn of the century, might well be useful to the tourist of today. "Personally, if I wanted to have an enjoyable cruise among the various island groups in the South Pacific I should avoid the 'excursion' steamer as I would the plague. . . . The appearance of a strange European in any of the environs of Apia is the signal for an onslaught of beggars of all ages and both sexes, who will pester his life out for tobacco; if he says he does not smoke, they say a sixpence will do as well. If he refuses he is pretty sure to be insulted by some half-naked ruffian, and will be glad to get back to the ship or to the refuge of an hotel. And yet, away from the contaminating influences of the town the white stranger will meet with politeness and respect wherever he goes."

Sketches in *The Strange Adventure of James Shervinton* (1902) are strongly autobiographical, and include "Pig-Headed Sailor Men," "Flash Harry of Savaii," and "Apinoka of Apamama," the potentate mentioned in Chapter One as an arms-buying, empire-building ruler of the Gilberts.

"Gun-Running in the South Seas," dealing with adventures during the Samoan civil war, also has the ring of veracity. In the same volume in which this sketch appears, *Under Tropic Skies* (1905), is found "The Pearlers," a terse narrative of a series of mishaps and brushes with cannibals at Kabaira Bay on New Britain which, if true, would qualify Becke as one of the most adventurous authors of his century.

The Call of the South (1908) has several sketches that are well worth recalling. "The Pit of Maota" is a terrible tale of the fate of four hundred and sixty-two villagers—men, women, and children —who had been captured during the Samoan civil war by their own people and cast alive into a blazing pyre. "My Friends, the Anthropophagi" gives personal recollections and historical accounts of blackbirding among the natives of the "Great 'Long Pork' Belt" of the cannibal South Seas. "On the 'Joys' of Recruiting 'Blackbirds' " is an account of one among the many episodes of labor-recruiting that Becke went through during his sea career.

The last book that Becke published in his lifetime, *'Neath Austral Skies* (1909), shows no falling off in his skill in recreating scenes from his Pacific past. "The Loneliness of It" recalls his favorite theme of the joys and worries of the trader's existence. "The Most Hateful Place I Know" is Hunter's Island, "a slumbering volcano, scantily wooded, waterless and uninhabited, rising almost sheer from the water's edge to over a thousand feet in height." On this isle (scene also of the climax of "The Trader's Wife"), where the sea boils a hundred yards off from the beach,

Becke and one friend were marooned for four days during a storm. "'Jack Shark'" returns to Becke's favorite theme of fishing, and of the dangers to white man and native alike from the hungry hunters of the depths and reefs.

Readers who browse among Becke's books can find for themselves many more favorite sketches from the Pacific. For twenty years he had been a keen-eyed, active observer and participant in a thousand episodes of South Sea life, and with an almost total visual recall was able to recreate such scenes. His pen did not falter even within a year or two of his death. He could still turn out a vivid recollection of the old days—but by then a new day had come and Becke's tales were now twice-told. He had finally satisfied the demand that he himself had created.

IV *An Australian on Australia*

Although born in the continent-wide nation of the South Pacific, Louis Becke is remembered more for his South Sea stories than for his accounts of Australia. Many of his writings, however, in fiction and in factual pieces, are set in his native country. He should not be classed with the school of "bush storytellers," and he never trumpeted any claims to being a "dinkum Aussie." Like most authors, he wrote best about what he knew best, and the fact is that he left Australia early and returned there only occasionally, between voyages to many other lands, for a year or two of various jobs ashore.

Rereading Becke's thirty-five books, one realizes that the range of continental settings is rather limited. He wrote much about the beaches and bush around Port Macquarie, his New South Wales birthplace, and about Northern Queensland, where he wandered as a prospector and roustabout, especially near Townsville and Charters Towers. Sydney, where he had spent a few years at school, was usually a starting-point or a terminus, like Auckland or Apia or many another port that he knew equally well. His association with Jeffery, as has been mentioned, plunged him deeply into Australian history, and his later work is full of colonial episodes. On his own he wrote novels like *Breachley, Black Sheep* and *Helen Adair* and *Tom Gerrard,* as well as novelettes like "Chinkie's Flat" and "The Settlers of Karossa Creek," set in Australia.

Although on the whole his writings about that region will be remembered less than his achievements in telling of things north of Cape York, some Australian pieces are well worth reading.

Among fictional treatments, E. C. Parnwell chose to select for his Oxford Classics volume, *Stories of the South Seas,* Becke's early tale of Queensland mining days, "The Great Crushing at Mount Sugar-bag," from *Pacific Tales* (1897). In his previous work, *The Ebbing of the Tide* (1895), Becke had included one Australian story, "Nell of Mulliner's Camp." *Rodman the Boatsteerer* (1898) contains "The Escapee," a story about a man on the Australian coast who is rewarded for befriending a fugitive from the convict colony of New Caledonia. Several Tom Denison stories have Australian settings; these are "Denison Gets a Berth Ashore" and "Denison's Second Berth Ashore," both in *Rídan the Devil* (1899), and "Denison Gets Another Ship," in *By Rock and Pool* (1901). In the former volume also appears one of Becke's most humorous stories, "Bilger, of Sydney," about an old cadger, a "mortuary bard" who sells obituary verse. Depiction of his growing grip on the victim approaches a Dickensian power.

Lack of demand for Australian stories, which others might be able to do as well as Becke, perhaps accounted for the fact that no others of this kind appeared in his books between 1901 and 1904, when *Under Tropic Skies* contained a good one, "The Traitor," about a North Queensland companion who is discovered to be a bandit.

"The Settlers of Karossa Creek" (1907), published by the Religious Tract Society, is a highly moral novelette about homesteading families that take up "selections" on the coast of northern New South Wales and come into conflict with a stubborn "squatter," or large landholder. Included are a sermon against swearing, a shipwreck, drought, bush fires, several love affairs, and an accusation of cattle-stealing, but the action is tamely juvenile. Included in the volume is a story of a family of smugglers in the same region, and a Tom Drake tale of how he befriended a Londoner crazed by a blow with a native war-club, and how the man was cured by a similar blow months later on the opposite side of his head.

Hard to classify or justify is the long piece, "Jim Trollope and Myself," in *The Pearl Divers of Roncador Reef* (1908). It is not a novelette, although some parts sound like fiction; nor is it clearly mere reminiscence of a vacation ashore for a few months in northern New South Wales, although the opening and some other incidents sound quite factual. The narrator, returning to his native haunts, picks up a fatherless sixteen-year-old lad who becomes his "mate" both on fishing excursions and in secretly extracting some gold dust from rich black beach sands, but little is made of Jim Trollope as a Huckleberry Finn of the bushlands. The pair baffle, by shooting a dog, a couple of wandering prospectors who try to find the secret diggings, and then join forces with another adventurer named Ross, with whom they prospect for gold on some inland creeks. But after a turn of luck, the storyteller, concluding with a couple of recollections of lonely periods on Pacific islands, breaks off after accepting an invitation to visit a married sister in Queensland. Some of the descriptions of hunting and fishing and chasing dingoes seem quite authentic, but this later work, along with two other pieces in the same volume ("A Prospecting Party in North Queensland" and "A Quick Vengeance," the latter describing the hanging of two gold robbers caught in the act of killing a pair of prospectors), do not add much luster to Becke's reputation as a writer on the placer-mining days in the northern part of his continent.

'Neath Austral Skies (1909) contains two more stories. "Julius Adolphus Jenkins's Christmas Alligator" concerns a conceited young city man who becomes a bank clerk in Townsville, and who cannot win his bride until he proclaims his manhood by shooting an alligator. This comedy contrasts strongly with the pathos of "Teresa Stuart," sole survivor of a Queensland family, who lives on as a slightly mad spinster talking to the ghosts of her lost ones.

Even the posthumous volume of 1913 contains one more Australian mining story, "The Prospector." But we must conclude that, except for parts of several novels and one or two novelettes, along with a handful of short stories, Becke without the aid of Jeffery did not write very much good fiction about Australia, and the settings for most of these come either from Sydney, northern New South Wales, or North Queensland.

Louis Becke was a shrewd, born student of the world about him, however, and a number of his nature notes concern the animals and marine life of his native land. His early and important non-fiction volume, *Wild Life in Southern Seas* (1897), opens with an exciting account of an attack off the coast of New South Wales upon a humpback whale by sharks and a "killer whale," who well deserves his name of *Orca Gladiator*. The narrative is made more dramatic because the observer's comments are supplemented by those of his six-year-old daughter, standing at his side on the headland. Two other non-fiction pieces are found in this volume: "On an Austral Beach" and " 'Leviathan' "—the latter an account of early whaling in the Southern Ocean, an occupation about which Becke knew more than a little.

Australian sketches are found in *By Rock and Pool* (1901). In addition to the title piece, "On a Tidal River" describes fishing near Port Macquarie, and "The Wily 'Goanner' " gives some account of the habits of the giant lizard, a favorite food of the aborigines. Three more sketches are found in *Yorke the Adventurer* (1901): "The Colonial Mortuary Bard," "The Black Bream of Australia," and "Five-Head Creek," an account of Becke's life as a cattleman for six months on a run west of Townsville.

A brief incident set in Becke's early home at Mosman near Sydney is recounted in "The Snake and the Bell," which appears in *The Strange Adventure of James Shervinton* (1902). Only one Australian sketch, "Dulce Est Desipere," is found in *Under Tropic Skies* (1904), but *Notes from My South Sea Log* (1905) includes such settings as well as those in parts of the South Pacific. This volume opens with one of Becke's best reminiscences—"Bay o' Fundy Days," describing his earliest home at Port Macquarie and the adventures of the Becke brothers in the neighborhood. It is followed by two more sketches from the same region, "The Pool the 'Greenbacks' Haunt" and "Night." *The Call of the South* (1908) includes two more sketches from this region—"A Recluse of the Bush" and "The Pattering of the Mullet." Finally, *'Neath Austral Skies* completes the list of recollections of northern New South Wales with "A Coastal Tramp"; "An Adventure with 'Grey Nurses' "—deadly sharks; and " 'Lots o' Time' "—another reminiscence of a Port Macquarie boyhood.

It used to be thought that *Old Convict Days* (1899), a full-length journal of the life of an Australian time-server who founded a respectable family, was written by Becke under a pseudonym. Becke did write an introduction under his own name for this book by one "William Day," but research has shown that the remainder was an authentic chronicle of the experiences of a certain William Derricourt—adventurer, convict, prospector, and solid citizen of his adopted land, Australia.

CHAPTER 7

Adventures in Assessment

WAS Louis Becke really the "prince of South Sea writers," "the Kipling of the Pacific," the best writer of tales of the Pacific Islands as they were during the nineteenth century?

Now that he has been lying in Waverley Cemetery for half a century, it is time to try to fix his place among those who have contributed to literature in English. It is difficult to do so because his work is voluminous and highly uneven. Agreement among even qualified critics is hard to find. His adventurous life was full of reefs and tides. His odyssey among the critics is almost as frequently filled with shoals and doldrums as with fair winds and snug harbors. It is necessary, therefore, to attempt to survey his literary reputation in England, America, and his native Australia, and then to summarize the main qualities of his work in fiction and non-fiction.

Part of Becke's appeal was his subject-matter. As he once wrote, "I received many hundreds of letters from men making inquiries as to how to get to the islands, cost of living, etc.; and they invariably wound up by some pointed questions concerning the ways of the Brown Woman."[1] Those dreamy escapists who sought a Polynesian paradise filled with free coconuts and free love were drawn by his yarns, even though he was a realist and made no attempt to seduce the imagination by appeals to the salacious. Indeed, he is almost always highly moral, and recognizes the needs of the spirit as well as the body. Louis Becke knew that man cannot live by breadfruit alone.

I *The Natural Man and Natural Woman*

One measure of a man's appeal is the reprinting of stories in anthologies. Becke was given the honor of an entire collection of his tales, and has been reprinted fairly often over the years.[2]

Becke has been seriously compared with Robert Louis Stevenson, Rudyard Kipling, and Herman Melville, and not always to Becke's disadvantage. A survey of critical comment over the past seventy years will reveal a variety of shades of opinion, but on the whole, the consensus shows that, with proper selection, Louis Becke is still worthy of a high place among the writers who dealt with the Pacific Islands and Australia.

It is inevitable to make a comparison between Becke and Robert Louis Stevenson, who did not come into the South Seas until 1888, just twenty years after Becke sailed on the *Lizzie and Rosa.* As Becke wrote, "More than a score of years before Robert Louis Stevenson went to die on the verdured slopes of Vailima Mountain, where he now rests, I was gaining my living by running a small trading cutter between the beautiful islands of Upolu, Savaii, and Tutuila."[3] R.L.S. died, having completed the writing of several volumes on the South Seas, the very year when Becke's first book appeared in London.

Becke himself admired Stevenson. "Now I love every line he wrote," he told a reporter for the London *Daily Chronicle* of August 5, 1896. "His 'Beach of Falesá' isn't a story; it's a photograph—a photograph of the white gleam of sandy beach, of sweeping surf, and waving palm."

Before his death, Stevenson read some of the stories of Becke, whom he called in a letter to Sidney Colvin a "howling cheese"—a cryptic but highly laudatory judgment.[4]

Commenting upon Stevenson's dedication of *Island Nights' Entertainment* to three supercargoes that Becke knew, he wrote in the *Pall Mall Gazette* in 1899: "The dust of the body of the master mind lies high up on Vailima Mountain, that of the two 'old shipmates' in the sand in Suwarrow and Funafuti lagoons. And if the shades of the dead do foregather, then one can imagine the thin finger of Stevenson beckoning to his old comrades of the Southern Seas, which he loved so well, to come to him and talk of those old, happy days spent in the cabins of the *Equator, Janet Nicol,* and the *Archer.*"

Becke wrote a letter of condolence to Fanny Van de Grift Stevenson, the widow, which was laid away among her "cherished possessions." Some time later, upon reading hints that Becke was to accompany Lord Rosebery in a South Sea cruise, Mrs. Stevenson wrote to urge that Samoa be included in the itinerary, but added: "If the rumor is an idle rumor, and without foundation, might I not hope that you, personally, may turn your face towards Samoa and those friends you have made with your pen who desire greatly to meet you? My husband, who took a keen interest in your work, had always wished to talk with you, but that, now, can never come to pass."[5] Another letter in the Dixson Library, from her son Lloyd Osbourne, was written to Becke from Dorking in the Samoan language, in which they were able to correspond.

The Stevenson family was more friendly toward Becke than the Stevensonian partisans in London. A reviewer remarked on November 13, 1897, in the London *Standard* concerning Becke's *Pacific Tales:* "If there had never been a Robert Louis Stevenson . . . the public would probably have paid much less attention to him [Becke] than he deserves. This is not saying that Mr. Becke is in any direct sense indebted to Stevenson, save, perhaps, for the title of one of his volumes."

Becke wrote to the editor of the *Standard* a letter appearing on November 17 to disclaim the implication that the title of his second book, *The Ebbing of the Tide* (1895), had been selected because of the popularity of Stevenson's *The Ebb-Tide* (1894). Becke made it clear that he had asked his publisher, Unwin, to choose the title, which came from an included story, "At the Ebbing of the Tide," published in the Sydney *Bulletin* two years before Stevenson's novel appeared.

The canard had apparently been floated by Edmund Gosse, arch-Stevensonian, with whom Becke had crossed verbal swords. As Becke wrote to Jeffery on May 16, 1897, "At a dinner given by Sir William Ingram the other day to a small party (16) among whom were Shorter, Dr. Nicol Robertson, Pemberton, Massingham and other big people, Conan Doyle asked me some question about South Sea matters. All the company waited to hear my answer. I referred Doyle to Gosse, who sat next to me (I hate the fellow's snobbishness) and said that since Stevenson was dead, Gosse was the only man who knew anything about the South Seas. I know I have made an enemy of him for life. . . . Just fancy the man having the damned cheek to suggest to me once at the Savile that I had taken my title 'The Ebbing of the Tide' from Stevenson's 'Ebb Tide.'"

Edward Reeves, on the other hand, was sorry that Stevenson and Becke never became collaborators. "Had they chanced to come together," he wrote, "what collaborateurs in such a work [on Bully Hayes] would have been Stevenson and the author of the brilliant stories in *By Reef and Palm,* 'Lui Becke,' who knew the Pacific as few men alive or dead have ever known it! Becke cruised with the pirate for a time in some ordinary trading expeditions, and must have heard in his wanderings more than he chose to tell of *his* collaborateur." [6]

Massingham, it will be recalled, on first seeing the stories sent by Becke from Sydney, wrote him that he thought them incomparably stronger than Stevenson's, "which seem to me clearly derived from them." Becke's fellow writers back on the Sydney *Bulletin* were loyal; one of them wrote on April 4, 1896, concerning "Louis Becke's New Book": "No one dreams of comparing his total achievement with Stevenson's, but in Becke's special sphere Stevenson is a weakling by comparison; all his art fails to reach the eloquence of Becke's simple touch of nature." Later critics have compared the two South Sea authors, not always to Becke's discredit. H. M. Green in his monumental *History of Australian Literature* (1961) concludes: "So far as concerns the sphere in which Stevenson and Becke overlap, Becke's range and understanding are much wider and more thorough, and he could do some things that Stevenson could not." (569)

The Earl of Pembroke, misled as he was by a sensationalized autobiography sent him by Becke, was his first critic in print, and in his introduction to *By Reef and Palm* (1894) was right in stressing its sometimes brutal realism. "Every one who knows the South Seas, and I believe many who do not, will feel that they have the unmistakable stamp of truth," he said of the tales (17), and later concluded: "But I think it is possible that the English reader might gather from this little book an unduly strong impression of the uniformity of Island life. The loves of white men and brown women, often cynical and brutal, sometimes exquisitely tender and pathetic, necessarily fill a large space in any true picture of the South Sea Islands, and Mr. Becke, no doubt of set artistic purpose, has confined himself in the collection of tales now offered almost entirely to this facet of life." (19–20)

A shrewd commentary was made by a reviewer of *Tessa and*

The Trader's Wife in the *Athenaeum* for August 17, 1901—a person who had visited Stevenson at Vailima: "Stevenson belonged heart and head to the North, and not at all to the Antipodes. . . . So Mr. Becke is hampered not merely by knowledge, but by actual touch with the raw facts themselves, over and about the whole range of which Stevenson's romantic imagination had free rein. When Mr. Becke draws upon the store aforementioned he generally presents his readers with good yarns, spontaneously rattled off, strong and ugly, but really valuable documents. In the other vein, of sentimentality, Mr. Becke ignores his store, draws upon tradition as he knows it, and presents his readers with mere sugary husks."

One can easily enjoy both Louis Stevenson and Louis Becke, without being invidious, for neither tried to rival the other on his own ground. It is, however, worth making the point that Stevenson, a highly civilized refugee from Europe, always saw the South Seas as a region of mystery and paradox, and only with great pain was able to make a home in the rain-forest heights above Apia. Becke was Pacific-born, and grew up doing jobs that at the time were not tinged with any sense of glamor. In a region which since the days of Rousseau had been identified as the haunt of noble savages, if such savages there were—in the setting traditionally chosen by hacks grinding out "South Sea stuff" to titillate the amorous dreamers yearning for the nymphs of Bougainville's New Cytherea—in an area almost synonymous with "romance," Becke was a regional realist.

Perhaps Mrs. Ingram's thesis puts, as well as it can be put, the distinction between R.L.S. and Becke. "Not for months, but for years did he [Becke] live among the natives; not as a Tusitala, a fascinating stranger, a man of wealth in a floating palace, did he visit them, but as a business man who lived and worked and played beside them. Not as an artist, consciously studying and analyzing their mode of life and customs did he question them, but as a companion, understanding and sympathetic—though with no great insight to carry him above and beyond his own observations—did he come to absorb a knowledge of their lives. The sincerity, simplicity, and interests of an intelligent man, possessed of a thorough knowledge of his subject, good sense, and a talent for spinning yarns, are reflected in his work." (97–98)

Rudyard Kipling, who greeted Becke on his arrival in London, was another writer with whom the Australian was compared. The interviewer for *Review of Reviews* of March 20, 1895, who mentions Becke's tribute to Stevenson in the Sydney *Town and Country Journal* a few days after the latter's death, says of Becke: "Now that Stevenson is dead, no one can write South Sea stories as he could—unless Kipling comes out to the islands for a cruise." An even more competent critic, who discussed *The Ebbing of the Tide* in the London *Saturday Review* for April 18, 1896, said of these two regional realists: "But if Mr. Becke cannot rival the craftsmanship of Mr. Kipling at his best, his successes in dealing with the life of the South Sea Islanders are not unworthy of being compared with the average level of Mr. Kipling's Indian stories; and the dazzling novelty of the primitive Pacific island life charms the reader so strongly that one would like to start forthwith in a pearling schooner for Pacific atolls and lagoons, expecting to rediscover a primitive Garden of Eden in which individual and social life are reduced to the very simplest elements. The natural man and, in particular, the natural woman are seen and painted by Mr. Becke with sympathy and fidelity, and this strange life appeals to us and stirs our curiosity until it becomes almost insatiable; and the chief charge that holds against Mr. Becke is that he has not given us more."

II *Becke's Friends the Americans*

Interesting is the little-known fact that Joseph Conrad, writing for Becke's publisher at the same time, envied Becke. "I am sorry to miss making the acquaintance of Mr. Becke," Conrad wrote to T. Fisher Unwin. "Strangely enough, I have been, only the other day, reading again his *Reef and Palm*. Apart from the great interest of the stories, what I admire most is his perfect unselfishness in the telling of them—the sacrifice of his individuality in the interest of the work. He stands magnificently aloof from the poignancy and humour of his stories; a thing I could never do—and which I envy him." [7]

S. R. Crockett, popular Scottish novelist, said in a letter of November 25, 1894, that Becke should not have had the bad taste to describe the flogging of a child in *By Reef and Palm*, even though the incident may have happened, but added: "For the rest I like

Becke. He tastes to me like Valtelline wine—rich of the soil, heady, rough; a vintage to be improved by keeping. I like all he writes and want more; it is my kind of reading."

The crest of Becke's English critical reception came when he published *Pacific Tales* (1897), and his scrapbook is laden with many favorable reviews. Among these the most penetrating is one entitled "Tragedies of the Pacific Seas" in *The Graphic* for 1897, written by T. P. O'Connor, M.P., renowned as "Tay Pay": "He [Becke] has the immense credit of having introduced to English readers an entirely new world. There have been, of course, plenty of stories of the Pacific Islands and seas—some of Robert Louis Stevenson's best work deals with the theme. But Mr. Becke, nevertheless, is the pioneer of the domain of fiction, and is still able to give to the world, periodically, tale after tale—wonderful, original, sometimes beautiful, sometimes grotesque. Mr. Becke has studied human nature in perhaps the very worst school through which human nature, in modern times, at least, has passed."

"Story-fish grow scarcer in Louis Becke's waters; and he is forced to use a smaller mesh and make a wider cast" runs a paragraph of June 24, 1899, on *Rídan the Devil.* On the other hand, a lengthy review of the same book in *Literature* for June 3, 1900, puts Becke in the category of sea writers with Kipling, Bullen, Conrad, and W. W. Jacobs, and concludes: "At his best Mr. Becke tells a story or relates an experience with a vigour and finish that are admirable, and in some half-dozen tales of the present collection he is at his best. But, first-rate as some of these stories are, the rest of the sketches that go to make up the volume are mere careless journalism, not devoid of lapses both in grammar and taste."

The boy who left school at fourteen sometimes horrified the London reviewers by such lapses, but his masters at the Fort Street Model School had given him a good start in composition and penmanship,[8] and his further education in the editorial office of the Sydney *Bulletin* had given him a mastery of ready prose. The "lapses" seem rather trifling in these days of permissible idiom. A review in the *Literary World* of July 23, 1897, said: "It is indeed strange to find Mr. Becke disfiguring his pages with mistakes most schoolboys could correct," and gives as examples the use of "us white men" and "like" in place of "as." But in humorous response to this charge Becke wrote: "I must plead as my excuse that 'I was never taught no grammer'—I had no chance of learning its simplest rules. And had I let this lack of knowledge worry me I would never have earned a stiver at literary work." [9] He was also frank to admit his lack of grounding in English literary schooling: "I went away from home when I was thirteen, with no knowledge of the outside world, and up to about four years ago I had only heard vaguely of such folk as Macaulay and Thackeray. Stevenson I never heard of till the *Bulletin* people told me that there was such a man who was writing of the South Seas." [10]

Carping continued in a note on *By Rock and Pool* (1901), which accuses Louis Becke of "pandering to the B.P. [British Public?] with his tongue in his cheek" and predicts that "few can write so much as he, and continue to write well." Irritation erupts in the *Athenaeum* of March 19, 1904, in a review of *Chinkie's Flat:* "Regarded from the literary standpoint, the author's work is simply exasperating, revealing as it does a very rich fund of material, handled with reckless carelessness and disrespect for the rules of grammar and for the elements of literary construction."

A year later, however, in the redoubtable *Quarterly Review,* Edward Wright in a lengthy article on authors who were dealing with outposts of empire said: "As a chronicler Mr. Becke is indeed excellent. He has taken up the story of the South Seas at the point at which Herman Melville laid it down. . . . Less impressive but more entertaining are the tales of shipwreck and adventure among buccaneers, cannibals, and missionaries—to place the objects of Mr. Becke's aversion in their ascending scale." [11]

Louis Becke knew and liked Americans. One of his earliest recollections was the arrival of the crew of the wrecked sperm-whaler *Adventurer* of Sag Harbor at Port Macquarie. The boy was so excited by the news that he took a short cut down the cliffs and fell sixty feet to the beach, where he was found some hours later with a sprained ankle and a fractured arm. He was consoled by the company of the captain and mate of the ship, who stayed for two months in the house. Some years later he again met Captain Devine, this time in Honolulu.[12] On his early voyage to Lord Howe Island, Louis met some other whalemen, and as he wrote: "Some years later, when I made my first four months' cruise in a New Bedford sperm-whaler, the theoretical knowledge I had gained on Lord Howe Island proved very useful to me." [13]

It is notable that Becke's first voyage to a foreign country landed him in San Francisco, where he claimed later to have met General W. T. Sherman.[14] In his semi-autobiographical *Adventures of Louis Blake* he describes voyages out of San Francisco to Lower California. He undoubtedly encountered many Americans in the South Seas. Merely during his brief stay on Kusaie, before the *Leonora* was wrecked there, he met the crews of two Yankee whale ships, as well as the resident Congregationalist missionary, Mr. B. G. Snow. His stories are sprinkled with American characters, good and bad. And, of course, his buccaneer hero Hayes was born in Cleveland, Ohio, and began his nefarious career as a "Great Laker."

Almost all of Becke's writing appeared in the United States as well as in the British Empire, and he had an eye always toward the American market. He wrote to Jeffery on May 20, 1897, that Lippincott had declined quite rightly to print *The Mutineer* in the United States, having said candidly that *His Native Wife* was so unfavorably received in America that they would run no more risks. ". . . I quite expected a storm to ensue as *His Native Wife* is so antagonistic to American missionaries that another book by the same author would get a chill reception." [15] He also admitted on November 24 of that year that there were parts of "The Tapu of Banderah" that the "Yanks would not like." But he urged later that Jeffery turn his research talents toward an article which later appeared under the title of "The Americans in the South Seas." [16]

Mark Twain was apparently the earliest American to appreciate Becke. During an interview given in Sydney on his lecture tour in 1895, Twain said: "And the chief charm of Louis Becke's stories for me is that the author seems to be chronicling facts and incidents he's seen—things he's lived amongst and knows all about." [17]

The popularity in America of the "local color" variety of fiction, in which regional characters, setting, and dialect assured the reader that he was living in a world of amusing or startling differences, attracted interest in Becke along with such other Pacific writers as Charles Warren Stoddard, author of *South-Sea Idyls* (1873) and other volumes. "Curiously enough," remarked a Sydney interviewer, "the American critics, who are generally so bitterly averse to what are known as 'color stories'—those dealing with colored races—speak very enthusiastically of his work, and say that in America he has but one rival—George Cable, author of *Old Creole Days* and *Madame Delphine*." [18]

Becke later met Cable in London, and was also, as has been mentioned, a close friend of Harold Frederic, about whom Becke wrote in a touching obituary: "The world of letters and journalism will long remember the big, burly American, with the rugged face and gruff voice. . . . His rough, bubbling humor, his generous sympathy to all literary beginners, and his savage outspokenness concerning anything which he considered was wrong or dishonest will never be forgotten by those who possessed either the privilege of his friendship or were subjected to the lash of his tongue, or the bitter satire of his pen." [19]

III *A Prophet in His Own Country*

Another endearing relationship between Becke and American literature is his bold recognition of Herman Melville, his predecessor in the South Sea islands, at a time when almost no Americans even knew the name of their great novelist. Two decades before the Melville revival began in 1921, Becke wrote a glowing introduction to a London edition of *Moby Dick*, commending the author as "the one man who knew his subject and knew how to write about it. . . . His writings possess that power and fascination that no other sea-writer, excepting Marryat, can exercise. He was of the sea; he loved it. Its hardships, its miseries, its starvation, its brutalities, and the grossness and wickedness that everywhere surrounded him in his wanderings through the two Pacifics, held but little place in the mind of a man who, ragged and unkempt as was too often his condition, had a soul as deep and wide and pure as the ocean itself, a soul that forever lifted him up above all mean and squalid things." He referred to Melville as "a born whaleman, a sailor, and a 'perfect gentleman,'" and summed up *Moby Dick* by saying: "I am no critic of literary 'style,' and only attempt thus poorly to express my opinion—that of a scantily educated seaman—of what I regard as one of the best 'sea-books' ever written." [20]

In return, many American critics have known and admired Louis Becke as a great writer about the sea. Thirteen years after Becke's death, a revival of interest was started by a short tribute, "Legend of Adventure," by Alan Rinehart. Knowing little about

Becke's life but wanting to know more, Rinehart states: "Most men write literature of one paltry sort or another; flimsy stuff; but Becke wrote in fiction the record of a quarter of the world, and his tales are all that remains of the lives of millions." [21]

Another American paid an early tribute in a monograph. Victor Riesenfeld concluded: "No lover of adventure, or seeker after knowledge of bygone times, can fail to include in the books he loves to read the works of Louis Becke, to whom the Pacific Isles and its peoples were as an open book, and who knew them better and loved them more than ever did any other man." [22]

The first American to recognize Becke's permanent worth was Dr. Carl Stroven, who created the unique course at the University of Hawaii in "Literature of the Pacific." He first offered it in the summer of 1935 under an eight-line description mentioning the study of "narratives by Melville, Loti, Stoddard, Stevenson, Becke, and other writers deserving, but less well known." In 1937 Dr. Stroven supervised a Master of Arts thesis by Margaret Anne Ingram, an early survey using typewritten materials kindly supplied by the Mitchell Library but omitting some of the facts of Becke's life that Mrs. Ingram might not have guessed or did not choose to include.

An early tribute to Becke by James A. Michener is worth quoting: "I have read some ninety books about certain small areas of the Pacific, and none gave me the pleasure that I found one rainy week in the Wallis Islands when my host had some half dozen prosaic books by Becke. They were, I must admit, poorly written, but they had upon them the stamp of allure, and they allure me still: the books of an unlettered man, a graceless storyteller, but a wonderfully tactile writer. I commend Becke highly." [23] When Michener asked me in 1954 to collaborate with him on a volume of biographies of ten colorful characters from Pacific history, Louis Becke was awarded a chapter and was also our main source of information on another chapter dealing with Bully Hayes the buccaneer.[24] Our concluding question is still unanswered: "What other author born and brought up in the Pacific region in the nineteenth century is better than Becke?"

As a sample of American appreciation in a scholarly study, *Ishmael* by Dr. James Baird may be cited as containing several important pages on Becke. "The twenty-three years of his voyages," writes Dr. Baird, "appear in an extensive sequence of tales and sketches which make the Polynesian romances of Melville, Stoddard, and Loti, in comparison, thin and inadequate as representations of native life. As a student of the Oceanic temperament, he is authoritative; as an observer of insular existence he has, more than any of his contemporaries, an accurate knowledge of the native mind, of what happens in it, of the dimensions which set it apart from the mentality of civilization."[25]

Louis Becke has not been without honor in his own country, despite the old attitude of humbleness that assumed no Australian could write anything comparable in value to anything written by a Londoner—the attitude described by one critic as the "cultural cringe." His companions in Sydney wrote loyally in the *Bulletin* of April 4, 1896: "Becke is, of all things, alive, vivid, vital. His characters leap at you from the printed page." Just before he departed for England, this journal hailed him as the possible leader of an "Australian literary Renascence."

A. T. Saunders in 1914, seeking factual information on Bully Hayes in the works of Louis Becke, placed too much reliance on the Earl of Pembroke's introduction to *By Reef and Palm* and failed to allow for Becke's penchant for fictionizing his experiences.[26] The bitter complaints of Saunders are offset by the tribute of S. W. Powell, an Englishman who had spent some years in the South Seas. Powell, in an undated letter to the Sydney *Morning Herald,* claimed that Becke wrote with far more knowledge of the Pacific than Melville or Stevenson. "But Australia has, it seems, determined to forget Becke. The oblivion which has been accorded him here is the more remarkable, because outside Australia, wherever the English language is read, he is recognized as the prince of South Sea writers. . . . But, after all, in the Australian attitude to Becke one sees only another illustration of the Biblical adage."

The invaluable two-volume pioneer study, *Australian Literature,* by E. Morris Miller gave Becke generous treatment on several pages, concluding that "Becke's claim to recognition as a writer rests mainly upon his innumerable short stories." Colin Roderick, in his *Introduction to Australian Fiction,* gave Becke several paragraphs, avowing that he was "a good story-teller," but "had no idea of developing a character or working out a sustained plot." At about this same time, the Australian author Rex Ingamells, discussing "Novelists of the Pacific," lengthily compared Becke with Stevenson and Melville, and proclaimed: "If Melville still stands as the foremost writer specifically concerned with the South Seas, Becke stands alone and unassailed as the most prolific writer of essential merit. Even when he romanticizes his facts, as occasionally he does, his romanticism emanates from a sound knowledge of the islands, and its spirit is authentic in a sense denied, for example, to the later, likewise prolific Beatrice Grimshaw, whose stories do not provide the same measure of conviction that life is 'like that' in the South Seas.

"Becke's subjects were frequently the very riff-raff which Melville despised; and, considering the different nature of his themes, Becke was, like Melville, a pioneer. He was the first adequately to portray the changed Pacific and circumstances which Melville could foretell but not describe; he wrote of practically nothing but island life, of that always interestingly: he was as picturesque and colorful as could be desired, but preserved the impression of reality; and in stories in which Europeans and natives are continually rubbing shoulders, Becke has yet no peer."[27] Lew Priday in the Sydney *Bulletin* of June 15, 1955, and several other Australians have given Becke a deep appreciation based upon a closer scrutiny than any American would be bold enough to apply.

However, there still remains some uncertainty among Australians as to Becke's place in their national literature. The most recent standard histories, published in the same year, are in strong contrast. H. M. Green's *History of Australian Literature* gives five large pages to Becke's work, both with and without his collaborator Walter Jeffery.[28] On the other hand, *Australian Literature*, by Cecil Hadgraft, admittedly a one-volume treatment, did not have room even to mention Becke's name.[29] There are many signs, however, that Becke is coming to be more widely appreciated in his own land.

IV *Laureate of a Violent Ocean*

In conclusion, an attempt will be made to summarize the qualities of Becke's work which have been discussed previously in detail.

Becke's non-fiction, especially his reminiscences and sketches, follows the "plain style" he learned as a Sydney journalist. Usually the choice of a first-person attitude lends a chatty authenticity to his remarks. One feels that here is a man who talks about what he knows and knows what he talks about.

Most of the qualities of Becke's stories, novelettes, and novels have already been mentioned. His themes are usually unpretentious, and boil down commonly to "life is like that." He favors courage and decency, but avoids preaching and didacticism. His philosophy, if it can be called that, ascends to no high theory-spinning. As an old sailor with whom I collaborated once told me, "We shellbacks of the windjammer days are sometimes criticized for lack of initiative and for counting too much on chance. But when you are depending on wind-power to get your ship around the world, you get the habit of trimming your sails and waiting for a breeze. You can't hurry the tide, and you can only hope for a lucky wind to fill your sails." Louis Becke was a sailorman, and luck or opportunism formed an important part of his outlook. He would work hard and cheerfully at the job at hand, but hope to whistle up a favorable wind that would bring him luck tomorrow.

The characters in his stories are often heroic but are sometimes drifters, weaklings, or gamblers. Their motives are usually far from profound. But they are frequently people of action, often violent action, and most of them do not suffer patiently under insult, boredom, or dishonor. They are not romanticists. As one of them says: "It is a foolish thing not to kill wounded men; they may get better and kill you." [30] Heroes and villains often come from the same groups that Becke knew so well—seamen, beachcombers, traders, pearl-shell seekers, missionaries, and natives of many lands. Becke's best-known creation, based on early personal acquaintance, was Captain Bully Hayes, bearded buccaneer and barrator, a dashing, heavy-fisted rogue with redeeming qualities that enabled the reader vicariously to share the bygone joys of roving the wide Pacific with a fierce freedom and disdain of the law unknown in these well-policed later days.

Although Becke had three wives and three daughters to observe, he, like Mark Twain, also a family man, was not ordinarily happy in realistically depicting the qualities of genteel femininity. On the other hand, his familiarity with brown girls of a hundred

South Sea islands, the Nadees and Niabons, enabled him to depict them as human beings, with intuitions, passions, and individual natures that make his white women, even when devoted sweethearts or faithless flirts, seem dreary by comparison.

Becke's plots, except when he worked on *The Mutineer* with Jeffery, often lack strong unity, especially in the longer forms of fiction. Limitations of scene and cast of characters also limited the devising of plausible plots, and when Becke did not feel strongly the special conflict in the story, he often fell back on the conventional plots of his Victorian competitors. The conflicts are usually on the physical level, man versus the forces of nature or man versus man using cunning or else brute personal violence and bullets. Occasionally man faces the enmity of society, but there is seldom great mental or psychological struggle, or conflict between man and supernatural forces, although the power of superstition is recognized. Becke has been accused of lacking plot altogether or else, in the words of H. M. Green quoted in Chapter 3, "He is never at a loss for a dramatic climax; indeed his climaxes appear perhaps a little too regularly." Probably the greatest value of Becke's plots is to buttress his realistic appeal. As pointed out in Mrs. Ingram's thesis, "His very defects in plot construction become paradoxically an element in his strength, for reading a number of his best tales gives one an unmistakable impression of trueness to life and of actuality, in spite of their strange and sometimes almost incredible adventures or crimes." (77)

Becke's most powerful quality is his evocation of the South Sea settings that he knew so well. He can be easily classed as a regional realist or a local-colorist. Theme, characterization, and action are often chosen to fit the particular stage where his figures find themselves, ranging from the open sea in a hurricane to a battle with cannibals in a palm-fringed lagoon. Yet Becke usually avoids static scene-painting or descriptive set-pieces; the place is part of the story, and is usually sketched in abruptly and reinforced by dialogue and rapid action. Details chosen are ordinarily significant emotionally, and appeal to various senses other than the visual—we get the unforgettable aroma of drying copra and the briny tang of the sea during a tropic dawn. With few words, the typical story starts out like this: "More than twenty years ago a fine young Polynesian half-caste, named Alan, and the writer were running a small trading cutter out of Samoa, among the low-lying atolls of the Ellice and Tokelau Groups, in the South Pacific."[31] The story goes on from there, in terse, fact-packed phrases. In longer works, scene shifts are often abrupt, and Becke leaps from episode to exciting episode, skipping all the dull days between.

Becke's strength, then, lies in his self-confidence born of the early experience of a writer who not only responded to the call of adventure, but viewed the scene as a man does who looks up from his labor to wipe the sweat from his forehead. The glamor has faded under the pressure of work, sudden hardship, illness, and bitter monotony, and the islands of the Pacific are shown to be real places on our planet, not the dreamlands of more artistic craftsmen such as Conrad, Stevenson, and Melville. This is the way it was.

Becke's style in narrative is much the same as that in his non-fiction—a style learned in the hard school of the Sydney *Bulletin*, avoiding the flowery or the finespun. His diction is rather limited, although he achieves a striking simile now and again, and as has been mentioned, he sometimes suffered from dialect trouble. His dialogues are often used for covering past or contemplated actions, seldom for utterance of subtle emotions. He is often capable of humor, pathos, gaiety, somberness, irony, and satire, and his style does not lack variety, for it changes slightly to fit the needs of the story and the expectations of the audience. However, Becke never aimed at the subtleties of a Henry James; he would be more likely to agree with Frank Norris's demand at the turn of the century: "We don't want literature; we want life!"

Becke's body of work is uneven, as previously pointed out, and requires critical selection; but his achievement did not decline after his first few books, and some of those written a decade later show no waning of his powers. At his best, Becke is superb. He is indeed the master of the short tale of the South Seas as they used to be. So long as readers seek to know from first-hand recollection and story-spinning the bygone life of the nineteenth-century Pacific region, so long will Louis Becke not be forgotten.

Notes and References

Chapter One

1. James A. Michener and A. Grove Day, *Rascals in Paradise* (New York, 1957), 249.

2. An autobiographical note in Becke's own hand is in the possession of the Mitchell Library, Sydney. It was sent to the Earl of Pembroke to form the basis of the introduction to Becke's first book. It is a fascinating but not altogether trustworthy document, containing errors and exaggerations, and must be used in connection with supporting materials. Note that nowhere does Becke give a single date. Because of its importance, it is here printed in full for the first time.

Am Australian born—native place, Port Macquarie, a little seaport town on the eastern coast of Australia. My father was Clerk of Petty Sessions there. Both he and my mother were English. My mother's father was private secretary to the then Duke of Cumberland, but inheriting some money he bought a small vessell and brought his family out to the colonies.

When I was about 14 my longing to go to sea was so intense that I gave my parents no rest upon the subject. At this time, however, an uncle of mine offered to send me and my brother Vernon (2 years older) to California, where we would be placed in a mercantile house. We were only too eager and shortly afterwards sailed for San Francisco in a wretched old French barque (no steamers to California in those days). The voyage was a terrible one. For over a month we were drifting about the Pacific, between New Zealand and the Australian coast, a partially dismasted and leaking wreck. The crew mutinied—they had bitter cause to—and only after calling at Rurutu in the Tubuai group and obtaining fresh food did they consent to the captain resuming command of the half-sunken old crate. In ninety days we reached Honolulu, and in 40 more the coast of lower California.

The routine of a merchant's office proving very distasteful to both my brother and myself the latter went into employment on a cattle ranche, and I obtained a berth in a clerical capacity in a steam service company. A year or so of this and I had money enough to take my passage in a schooner bound on a shark-catching cruise to the islands of the North Pacific. C.J and P. The life was a very rough one and the cruise full of incident and adventure. Returning to Honolulu I fell in with an old man who had bought a schooner for a trading venture among the Western Carolines. I put in $1000 and we sailed. He and I were the only whites on board. I was supercargo. I soon found out that although he was a good seaman, he could not navigate. In a few weeks we were among the Marshalls and the old captain who had been drinking heavily went mad from D.Ts. We (three native sailors and myself) ran the vessel into a little uninhabited atoll, and for a week had to watch the captain closely from committing suicide. At last we got him right and stood away to the w. Soon afterwards we fell in with a big Marshall Island sailing canoe. She had been blown away from Arnu and had drifted 600 miles to the westward. Seventy people had been her complement, of these 30 had died. We gave them water and provisions and left them to make Strong's Island which was then in sight 40 miles off. Before leaving the Chief and I swore Marshall Isd. bruderschaft. Years afterwards when I came to live in the group he showed his friendship for me in a signal manner. Our voyage proved a profitable one, and from that time I determined to devote myself to trading. Returning to California I took passage to Samoa and after some experience there back to Sydney. Just at this time the Palmer River Gold Rush (North Queensland) had just broken out. A brother of mine who was bank manager at an adjacent gold field wrote me to come up—everyone was making a fortune. I spent two years on the gold-fields and on a cattle station, did not make a fortune, but gained plenty of experience that proved of service to me. Returning to Sydney I learnt blacksmithing and became a crack rifle shot. I remained only a few weeks and then sailed for the Friendly Islands. I intended settling down there as a trader but the morose character of the natives disenchanted me. Went on to Samoa and bought a cutter and traded in partnership with a Manihiki half-caste throughout the group. Col. Steinberger was at this time in the zenith of his brief tenure of power and the natives were fighting. During this two years' residence I made a study of the language and sought to learn all I could of the native character and mode of life. From Samoa I was sent away in charge of a small trading vessel under sealed orders to the Marshall Islands. My orders were to hand this vessel over to the notorious Bully Hayes (I will not weary your lordship in a letter with the details of this very curious adventure). Hayes was awaiting me in Milli Lagoon. I handed over my charge to the famous "Bully" and then taking passage with him for my return to Samoa was wrecked with him in the brig "Leonora." Hayes made himself ruler of the island and he and I had a little quarrel. After some very exciting incidents Hayes was captured by an English man-of-war but escaped. I returned to the Colonies in the cruiser. Went back again to Eastern Polynesia, Gambiers, Paumotus, Easter and Pitcairn Island, picked up an abandoned French barque on a reef, floated her, loaded her with coconuts and attempted to sail her with a native crew to N. Zealand. Went ashore in a hurricane and lost everything. Then went as supercargo to a Liverpool firm to the Ellice and Tokelau groups. Remained with them some years and finally settled in the Ellice Group as a trader. Made some money and took passage for the Caroline Group. Vessel was wrecked on Peru Island in the Gilbert Group—lost every dollar I had in the world. Returned to Samoa and engaged as "Recruiter" in the labour traffic. Got badly hurt during an encounter with the natives and went to N. Zealand to recover. Sailed again for New Britain on a trading venture. My adventures here were exciting enough. A bad attack of malarial fever and a wound made me leave and return to the Marshall Islands. From there I returned to the colonies for a few weeks and then again found myself back in the Islands on a guano-prospecting voyage. From then till about two years ago I have been living on various islands, leading a wandering and lonely yet not unhappy existence. I do not wish to write what may seem egotistical to your lordship but I think I may venture to assert that in all my wanderings and researches I have been a favored man with the natives and "Lui," as they call me, is well-known from Easter Island to the Pelews and the brown people would like to see me back among them again. Years ago the people of Nanumaga named me *Fana tonu* (True-shot) and this name also has stuck to me.

Becke's family called him "Nunka," which according to his daughter Niya in a letter to me of December 31, 1963, was given him by South Sea natives and means "my best friend." An undated letter from London sent by Fanny Sabina Becke to her daughter Alrema suggests that the Becke family had Norman blood going back to William the Conqueror, when Walter Bek came to England in 1066. Walter's three sons founded great Lincolnshire families, one being Bek of Eresby, whom Louis Becke claimed as a forbear. He spoke to his family of relationship with Anthony Bek or de Beck, Baron of Eresby and Bishop of Durham, the site of whose fourteenth-century mansion on the banks of the Thames is now the Adelphi district. Becke also claimed relationship with the Ancasters of Eresby, and for a time used a fancy crest on his notepaper.

3. "'Lots o' Time,'" in *'Neath Austral Skies*, 267.
4. Sydney *Bulletin*, February 27, 1913, 2.
5. "A Memory of the 'System,'" in *Ridan the Devil*, 27.
6. "Night," in *Notes from My South Sea Log*, 08.
7. Becke wrote of his boyhood in "'Bay o' Fundy Days'" (*Notes from My South Sea Log*) and "'Lots o' Time'" (*'Neath Austral Skies*). A London publisher was so impressed with the first of these pieces that he suggested to Becke that the setting would be a good one for a book for young people.
8. *Old Convict Days*, vii.
9. See "The Tanifa of Samoa" in *By Rock and Pool*.
10. "The True Story of the 'Real' Bully Hayes," manuscript in Sir Alexander Turnbull Library, Wellington, p. 11.
11. John Daniel Fitzgerald, *Studies in Australian Crime*, 1st series (Sydney, 1924), 115.
12. *Daily News*, London, August 15, 1896.
13. All the surviving letters are in the Mitchell Library. An inter-

viewer in the London *Daily News* for August 15, 1896, wrote: "I may say that for many years Mr. Becke has written long letters home to his mother. These were fortunately preserved, and have furnished him with much material. Diaries and journals are not easy for wanderers to keep, but Mr. Becke is a persistent 'logger'—they call journals 'logs' out there. He has, moreover, an excellent memory."

14. In *Mid-Pacific* (Boston and New York, 1926).

15. Winchcombe got his revenge in his diary, now in the possession of the Mitchell Library, in which he wrote: "An English man Lewis Becke arrived here May 7, 1881, in the schooner Redcoat to await the arrival of another vessel to take him to the Line Islands. The natives were not at all anxious about his landing here from some previous tidings of him about the islands and offered him no accommodation he therefore went to Teacher's house and soon made arrangements to land here and to live with the teacher. . . . Amongst other things were about 50 Guns with ample ammunition and about 30 cases Liquor, here he remained sevl weeks passing his time by fireing guns day after day and greatly disturbing the peace of the island, we visited each other occasionally and I purchased few articles of him in the Teachers house and drank grog there with him." Adds Philip Gallagher, who found this entry: "Becke and Winchcombe evidently did not part on the best of terms. Becke later put his drinking mate in a story, 'Tarria, the Swimmer,' as 'Winchcombly' and had him murdered in a San Francisco tavern."—Sydney *Morning Herald*, August 15, 1953. In this story, which appeared in the *Bulletin* for June 22, 1911, Winchcombly is termed "a drink-besotted, unclean creature, illiterate and violent-tempered."

16. The Becke despatch box in the Mitchell Library contains a typewritten letter from W. Telfer Campbell, Deputy Commissioner, Gilbert and Ellice Islands, Betio, 9th October, 1900, to C. R. Swayne, Esq., Nadrulolo, Fiji, as follows:
"Sir,
"I have the honour to forward herewith, in compliance with your request, a certified extract relating to a marriage performed at Nukufetau, Ellice Group, between Louis (Becke) and Nelea, a native of Nukufetau." Fees for application in chambers and for affixing seal of court to the extract amounted to seven shillings and sixpence.

17. *Notes from My South Sea Log*, 264.

18. "Apinoka of Apemama," in *The Strange Adventure of James Shervinton*, 303.

19. See Josephine H. Niau, *Phantom Paradise* (Sydney, 1936), and James A. Michener and A. Grove Day, *Rascals in Paradise* (New York, 1957), Chapter II.

20. *Ridan the Devil,* 243.

21. Becke stated in an unpublished manuscript in the Sir Alexander Turnbull Library, "Fifty Years Ago: 'Old' Sydney Harbour," p. 5, written in 1911, that he had served as supercargo on the labor-recruiting brig *Iserbook,* owned by the famed firm of J. C. Godeffroy and Sons of Hamburg.

22. "Rolf Boldrewood," *A Modern Buccaneer* (London, 1894), 83.

23. Although Becke does not mention his marriage either in his "Autobiography" or elsewhere, the Earl of Pembroke in his introduction to *By Reef and Palm,* 15–16, states: "During one of his visits to the Colonies he married a young Irish lady, a daughter of Colonel Maunsell of H. M. 11th Regiment, by whom he has two children." A daughter, Nora, was born November 9, 1888, but was not baptized until September 13, 1903. Becke speaks often of Nora, and presumably took her to live with him on Niue or Savage Island (see "My Native Servants," 91, and "Niué," 283, in *Wild Life in Southern Seas*). Nora eventually married and lived for years in Portugal, where she died on October 12, 1962. Her father's obituary in a Port Macquarie newspaper in 1913 stated: "His daughter is a very distinguished linguist, and represented Great Britain at an international congress of languages held in St. Petersburg." Becke's dedication in *The Adventures of a Supercargo* is "To Nora Lois, my shipmate in Southern Seas." Concerning her younger brother, T. A. Browne, in a letter to Becke of March 14, 1894, says: "I sympathise most deeply with you and Mrs. Becke in the loss of your little boy."

24. See "Yacob and Pig" in *Notes from My South Sea Log,* 167.

25. Lew Priday, "Trader Becke of the South Seas," Sydney *Bulletin,* June 15, 1955, 25.

26. Sydney *Bulletin,* February 27, 1913, 2. Philip Gallagher in the Sydney *Morning Herald,* August 15, 1953, says that the Favenc-Archibald story is undoubtedly true, but "Becke was working as a journalist in Sydney for more than twelve months before his first article appeared in the 'Bulletin' in December, 1892." This conclusion is supported by my own search in the files. The unsigned article in the Christmas issue of the *Bulletin* (XII, December 24, 1892, 24), about the massacre of white vagabonds on Ocean Island in the 1850's, is in Becke's style. Another on January 21, 1893 (XII, 19), again unsigned, is based on "a letter received in Sydney from native sources" and mentions Bully Hayes and Ben Peese. Clearly Becke's work is "'Bully' Hayes: the Pirate of the Pacific," a two-part unsigned reminiscence appearing in the *Bulletin* in 1893 (XII, February 4, 22–23, and February 18, 21), reprinted with some modifications in *The Strange Adventure of James Shervinton* (London, 1902, 215 ff.). Such non-fiction appear-

ances at least four months before " 'Tis In the Blood" throw some doubt on the romantic account of Becke's "discovery" by Archibald as a short-story writer, and support the more usual view that even writers of high talent seldom burst upon the world without any sort of apprenticeship in the craft.

Chapter Two

1. Becke never claimed that they had met. Writing about Bully Hayes, he says: "At this time, the late Earl of Pembroke, the joint author with Dr. Kingsley of *South Sea Bubbles*, was in Apia Harbor in his schooner yacht *Albatross*." (*The Adventure of James Shervinton*, 237) The earl, in his introduction to *By Reef and Palm*, writes: "When in October, 1870, I sailed into the harbour of Apia, Samoa, in the ill-fated *Albatross*, Mr. Louis Becke was gaining his first experiences of island life as a trader on his own account by running a cutter between Apia and Savaii." But the earl was misled by notes supplied him by Becke, who in 1870 was a fifteen-year-old messenger boy in San Francisco.

2. See Chapter 1, note 2.

3. According to a certified copy of a birth certificate, Fanny Sabina Long was born on March 17, 1871, in the district of Uley in Gloucestershire, daughter of a sculptor, Samuel Beauclerc Long, and Fanny Arabella (Warner) Long. She was sixteen years younger than Louis and presumably a Sydney literary friend. Her daughter Niya wrote me that Sabina was not born in Queensland, as stated by one writer, "nor did she ever visit Queensland or accompany Louis on his wanderings along northern New South Wales beaches." As late as June 21, 1898, Becke in a letter from England to his collaborator Jeffery in Sydney referred to Sabina as "Nora's governess." A book contract between Becke and T. Fisher Unwin dated December 11, 1905, was witnessed at Becke's address, 11 Villa des Falaises, Le Havre, France, by one "Sabina Lewis."

Biographers sometimes confuse Bessie and Sabina. A divorce was granted to Bessie in Sydney in 1903, when the judge decided that notice could be served on the respondent even though he was then reputed to be in Jamaica, since he was a well-known person. Of Bessie, Becke's brother Vernon wrote on January 31, 1909 that she was "supposed to have kept an hotel at Balmain in the name of Stewart and had two young daughters."

Sabina helped Louis in his work and acted as typist and amanuensis. She also was a writer. In the Fiji *Times* for December 4, 1908, the interviewer remarks: 'Like her more noted husband Mrs. Becke wields a fluent pen and has been a contributor to the *Wide World Magazine*, the *Westminster Gazette,* etc., and is now engaged on a book of reminiscence."

Sabina died at the age of eighty-eight at Rye, East Sussex, on December 8, 1959, and was cremated at Charing, Kent, on the 14th. For some years previous she had been paid a pension by the Australian Commonwealth government as the widow of a distinguished author.

Two daughters were born of the union: Alrema or "Billie," on October 30, 1897, and Niya, who was given her mother's nickname, on September 27, 1898. Their father told them that Alrema meant "Morning Star" and Niya meant "Little One." Both were living in Springwood, N.S.W., Australia, in 1966; Alrema was the widow of a man named Hardie. The "Niya" to whom *Rídan the Devil* was dedicated is their mother. *Tom Gerrard* was dedicated "To Alrema" and *Under Tropic Skies* "To Tatoé," which was Becke's nickname for his daughter Niya. As she explains in a letter, she was unable when very young to pronounce "potato" properly, and "Tatoé" was her family name for many years. She followed her father into journalism, wrote verse, worked on the Sydney *Daily Telegraph,* published an article on Norfolk Island illustrated with her own photographs, and worked in London for a time as secretary in the firm of T. Werner Laurie, publishers.

4. Concerning De Wolf, Becke wrote to Jeffery on May 31, 1898: "He is my *one* great personal friend here in England. . . . I served under him as trader when he and his brothers lost £20,000 trying to establish a South Sea Island trading business on honest principles in antagonism to the great German firm of J. C. Goddefroy & Co. of Hamburg, the which robbed and swindled whites and natives alike."

5. Typescript, 24.

6. Typescript, 27.

7. Dixson Letters.

8. Typescript, 27.

9. Correspondence from all these persons appears in the Dixson Letters.

10. "Before this [1906]," Becke wrote in 1912, "I had written a tale of adventure (primarily for boys), called *Tom Wallis,* and placed it with my literary agent, who hawked it about from publisher to publisher for months. He could have sold it over and over again for a price that would have well satisfied me, but he wanted too much for it. I was then contributing short stories to the *Boys' Own Paper* and the *Leisure Hour;* and one day the editor of the latter asked me if I could give him a long serial. I thought of *Tom Wallis,* and managed to get the MS. back from the agent. Within three days the Religious Tract Society bought the serial rights for £210 for the *Leisure Hour* and the book rights for a similar sum. It had a great success. My agent

(who drew up the usual agreement with R.T.S.) netted his 10 per cent. commission although he had absolutely nothing to do with selling it. After that experience I became my own agent." Sydney *Bulletin,* February 27, 1913, 2.

11. See "London Notes" by Becke in Sydney *Evening News,* especially for December 8, 1898, and also Edward Clodd, *Memories* (London, 1916), 123.

12. Jamaica *Daily Gleaner,* August 8, 1902.

13. Quotations from Becke's Jamaica letters come from the collection of Dr. George Mackaness of Sydney, N.S.W.

14. Typescript, 28.

15. Letter in Mitchell Library.

16. Typescript, 31.

17. Sydney *Morning Herald,* February 19, 1913.

18. A tribute in verse at Becke's death was published in the Sydney *Bulletin* for February 27, 1913, written by Henry Lawson, one of Australia's great short-story writers, which is well worth preserving:

They're at their age-long harvest still—the angels Death and Time—
But ebb or flow we all must go and leave the broken rhyme.
Wide blue with white-caps here and there—the glory of the day
A space of seascapes wondrous fair, in Islands far away;
Faint silver on the distant reef, on skylines scarce a fleck
But fleecy clouds of blest-relief that welcome Louis Becke.

Who'll miss the well-known stuttering speech? Who'll mind the distant date
When by the mast and palm-fringed beach those halting words had weight?
Who'd dream those sad kind manly eyes when traders were in "holts"
In summer Isles of Paradise could glint behind a Colt's?
We only know *By Reef and Palm*—the world he made his own—
(The later wounds, without a balm, are better never known.)

We live and fight by day and night in carking care and strife
And take our pen in death to write the story of our life.
Farewell, my friend—'twill ne'er be told—or told in printed line
Your destiny in days of yore was strongly linked with mine.
I trust my track shall run as true, though it come late or soon,
When my name shall be missing, too, from "Some Birthdays in June."

Chapter Three

1. The requirements of the typical *Bulletin* story are admirably stated by H. M. Green in his early *Outline of Australian Literature* (Sydney, 1930), 106–107: "The *Bulletin* short story was on the average the shortest of all short stories. Sentences must be brief and words

must not be wasted; descriptive and explanatory matter must be cut to a minimum. Other requirements were simplicity, directness, realism, and dramatic pace. There was comparatively little in the way of fine shades and subtleties, and the imagination was kept well within bounds. Irony was reckoned decidedly among the virtues and, though pathos was by no means excluded, it had to stop short of sentimentality. The characters of the stories were on the whole a hard-bitten lot who had to face facts but facts also were commonly pretty hard; even in the humorous stories the atmosphere was sometimes rather grim. Both the characters and the framework of the stories were unconventional, sometimes startling if measured by the accepted standards of the day, but this meant merely that a new set of conventions had been substituted for the old. The subject matter within a certain range was extremely varied yet this range was somewhat narrow. Finally, the *Bulletin* story had in it a large element of the primitive." These qualities quite clearly describe most of Becke's earlier tales.

2. Sydney *Bulletin*, August 17, 1955, 2.
3. *Ibid.*
4. H. M. Green, *A History of Australian Literature* (Sydney, 1961), I, 568–69.
5. *Ibid.*, 569.

Chapter Four

1. Unidentified review, July 23, 1898, Large Scrapbook.
2. Fred Johns, *An Australian Biographical Dictionary* (Melbourne, 1934), 23.
3. See Geoffrey Rawson, *The Strange Case of Mary Bryant* (London, 1938) and Frederick A. Pottle, *Boswell and the Girl from Botany Bay* (New York, 1937, and London, 1938), both of which contain notes and appendixes. An account based on testimony at the Public Office in Bow Street, London, July 15, 1792, is found in manuscript in the Jeremy Bentham papers, University College, London, and reprinted in G. C. Ingleton, *True Patriots All* (Sydney, 1952), 13–15. A recent geographer, bemused by the solemn preface of Becke and Jeffery, has cited their imaginary sergeant as a primary source for the story: "A chart with the boat's track shown on it was preserved by a soldier on a British vessel which later took the survivors into custody. This soldier also preserved an account of the voyage by Mary Bryant. . . ."—Andrew Sharp, *The Discovery of Australia* (Oxford, 1963), 185. Becke presumably knew the tale long before he began work on the novel: "My mother had often told us the story of William Bryant," he says in "A Memory of the 'System'" (*Rídan the Devil*, 45–46). Of Mary Bryant, one author concludes: "It cannot be denied that with

her husband and other convicts she took part in the most wonderful open-boat voyage ever made, and certainly no European woman or child ever made such a voyage before or since that time."—Frank Reid, *The Romance of the Great Barrier Reef* (Sydney, 1954), 25.

The rare little book *Boswell and the Girl from Botany Bay,* by Frederick A. Pottle, is a charming retelling of the story and contains valuable documents which, had Becke and Jeffery known of them, would have provided an even more dramatic ending to their novel. Near the end of his life, the author of *The Life of Samuel Johnson* was an unsuccessful member of the English Bar, and had always interested himself in poor criminals whom no one else would defend. Probably through his efforts, Mary became a free woman, lived for a while in London on funds raised by Boswell, and as we learn through occasional references in his journal, was finally sent off to her homeplace at Fowey in Cornwall. A note on page 55 makes clear that although Boswell supplied Mary with funds, their connection was not an improper one.

4. *Introduction to Australian Fiction* (Sydney, 1950), 46.

5. H. M. Green, *History of Australian Literature,* 633n., credits *The Mystery of the Laughlin Islands* to Jeffery alone, although both Becke and Jeffery are named on the title page.

6. The list of writings on the *Bounty* mutiny is voluminous and still growing. For the ordinary reader, the best short account is still that in *The Life of Vice-Admiral William Bligh, R.N., F.R.S.,* by George Mackaness (Sydney, 2nd ed., 1951), containing a lengthy bibliography which includes Bligh's own versions of events. Invaluable for the nine-month period between the mutiny and the landing on Pitcairn is the monograph "In Search of a Home" by H. E. Maude (Smithsonian Institution *Report* for 1959, Washington, D.C., 1960, 533–62), which also contains an excellent bibliography. Maude, who lived on Pitcairn for nine months, uses forty-five sources on this period of the wanderings, but leans especially upon James Morrison's journal and on two accounts of a Tahitian woman named Jenny, who went to Pitcairn as the wife of Isaac Martin. A sociological study of the colony and its descendants which makes good reading is *The Heritage of the "Bounty"* by Harry L. Shapiro (New York, 2nd ed., softbound, 1962).

7. Becke gave one of his daughters this melodious name from the early novel.

8. Becke wrote Jeffery from Port Macquarie in March, 1896: "My idea is that by making Stewart and Heywood play Christian false we increased our hero's mental tribulations. I have also in Chapter 16 made Christian write a confession, which is destroyed by Young." This confession does not appear in the final version. A recent study, *Who*

Caused the Mutiny on the "Bounty"?, by Madge Darby (Sydney, 1965), supports Becke and Jeffery by accusing Edward Young of masterminding all the plots.

9. *Wild Life in Southern Seas*, 45–48. For a good recent account see Bengt Danielsson, *Love in the South Seas* (New York, 1956), Chapter 8.

10. Unidentified review, July 23, 1898, Large Scrapbook.

11. *My Island Home* (Boston, 1952), 310, 312.

12. Further search by Hall might have uncovered two earlier *Bounty* novels: Captain Frederick Chamier, *Jack Adams, the Mutineer* (London, 3 vol., 1838); and R. M. Ballantyne, *The Lonely Island; or The Refuge of the Mutineers* (London, 1880).

13. In a letter of June 13, 1899 (from Mackaness Collection) Becke wrote to Jeffery that the Phillip book had occupied much of his time "in consequence of Wilson's copious appendices. I have now read and passed for about four times 'the last revises.'"

14. In the Gregg M. Sinclair Library of the University of Hawaii.

15. Identification of authorship of all the stories in *The Tapu of Banderah* is now made possible by the discovery of a typewritten sheet in the Dixson Letters headed "List of Stories by Becke and Jeffery, to be used by C. Arthur Pearson, Ltd, in book (and serial) form," which indicates authorship by "B & J," "L B," and "W J." Comparison with the table of contents of the printed book shows a few changes in exact titles. Becke alone was author of "Sarréo," "Man and a Brother" (titled "The Brothers-in-Law" in the volume), "In the Far North," "The Brass Gun of the Buccaneers," "Pàkía," and "Susani." Jeffery alone was author of " 'The Gallant, Good Riou' " and "The Americans in the South Seas," a title not on the list; however, this latter sketch, which uses the phrase "the gallant, good Riou," is mentioned as his in Becke's letter of February 6, 1899. All the remaining seven stories, including the novelette "The Tapu of Banderah," were written in collaboration. Listed on the sheet is another collaborative effort, "Hori Grey," concerning Sir George Grey, which appeared in the *Fortnightly Review* but was omitted from the volume. In the June 13, 1899, letter to Jeffery (Mackaness Collection) Becke says: "I have sold per Watt a collection of our collaborated articles and stories to Pearsons, but the transaction is not complete owing to Pearsons asking me to substitute some new matter of my own in place of much of our joint work. This I have been unable to do hitherto, but am now doing."

16. *Free Lance*, Melbourne, June 18, 1896.

Chapter Five

1. For a bibliography, see James A. Michener and A. Grove Day, *Rascals in Paradise* (New York, 1957), 358–59.

2. "Concerning Bully Hayes" in *The Strange Adventure of James Shervinton,* 215–16.

3. See, for example, "The Kanaka Labour Trade in the Pacific" and "On the 'Joys' of Recruiting 'Blackbirds' " in *The Call of the South;* and "The Recruiters" in *Under Tropic Skies.*

4. " 'Lots o' Time,' " in *'Neath Austral Skies,* 267–272.

5. *Adventure,* New York, September, 1914.

6. *Bully Hayes, Buccaneer* (Sydney, 1913), 9–10.

7. "Some Skippers with Whom I Have Sailed," in *'Neath Austral Skies,* 165.

8. *Adventure,* New York, September, 1914.

9. A letter to Becke from Sidney, fourteenth Earl of Pembroke, dated September 28, 1896, states: "Mr. Browne's conduct was certainly most vexatious for you in spite of the implied compliment to your writing, and I do not see how you could have passed it over without remonstrance. . . . I saw a review of the 'Modern Buccaneer' and gathered that it was a biography of Hayes. I am afraid that it must have forestalled your intended book on the subject."

10. Although H. M. Green discusses Browne's five most important novels, he nowhere mentions, oddly, *A Modern Buccaneer.*

11. Hayes was borrowed by later novelists. He is the main character of two books by Albert Dorrington (*A South Sea Buccaneer,* Sydney, 1911, and *Our Lady of the Leopards,* Sydney, 1911) and appears in a novel by Will Lawson, *The Laughing Buccaneer* (Sydney, 1935). Robert Louis Stevenson had mentioned Hayes casually in *The Wrecker;* Edward Reeves in *Brown Men and Women* (London, 1898, 2) states that Stevenson could have used Hayes for a book better than *Kidnaped* or *Treasure Island.*

12. Most useful for this recounting, in addition to *A Modern Buccaneer,* are the following Becke essays: "Bully Hayes the Pirate," *Bulletin,* Sydney, February 14, 1893; "The Wreck of the *Leonora:* a Memory of Bully Hayes," in *Rídan the Devil* (London, 1899, 281–95); "Concerning 'Bully' Hayes," in *The Strange Adventure of James Shervinton* (London, 1902, 215–66); "A Memory of the Southern Seas," in *Chinkie's Flat* (London, 1904, 233–37); "The Real Bully Hayes," *Lone Hand,* Sydney, March 1, 1912, 378–88; "Bully Hayes" in *Bully Hayes, Buccaneer* (Sydney, 1913, 9–34); and letter to *Adventure* magazine, New York, September, 1914.

13. Unpublished manuscript in Sir Alexander Turnbull Library, Wellington, "The True Story of the 'Real' Bully Hayes," p. 2.

14. *The Field,* March, 1897.

15. "Leassé" in *Rodman the Boatsteerer,* 298–99. Other sketches concerning this period of dwelling among the unspoiled people of Kusaie include "An Island Memory: English Bob" and "The Shadows of the Dead" in *Pacific Tales;* "The River of Dreams," "Fish Drugging in the Pacific," and "The Deadly Oap" in *Yorke the Adventurer;* "Concerning 'Bully' Hayes" in *The Strange Adventure of James Shervinton;* "Adrift in the North Pacific" in *Notes from My South Sea Log;* "The Supercargo" in *Under Tropic Skies;* and "Bully Hayes" in *Bully Hayes, Buccaneer.*

16. The Reverend James Chalmers, passenger on the salvaged *John Williams,* although recounting several incidents that revealed Hayes at times acted "more like a madman than a sane man," admitted that on this passage Bully was "a perfect host and a thorough gentleman."—*Autobiography and Letters,* edited by Richard Lovett (Oxford, 1902), 67. H. Stonehewer Cooper wrote: "Captain Hayes . . . had a charming manner, dressed always in the perfection of taste, and could cut a confiding friend's throat, or scuttle his ship with a grace which, at any rate, in the Pacific, was unequalled."—*Islands of the Pacific* (London, 1888), II, 64. Edward Reeves, who knew Hayes in New Zealand in the sixties, wrote: "He was a stout, bald, pleasant-looking man of good manners, chivalrous, with a certain, or rather uncertain, code of honor of his own—loyal to anyone who did him a good turn; gentle to animals, fond of all kinds of pets, especially of birds."—*Brown Men and Women* (London, 1898) 5. Charles Elson, mate of the little ship *Lotus* on which Hayes met his death at the age of fifty, concluded: "Despite his evil life Hayes carried something big in his soul. . . . He might have attained an honorable career had he but learned self-discipline early in life."—A. T. Saunders, pamphlet, "Bully Hayes: Barrator, Bigamist, Buccaneer, Blackbirder, and Pirate" (Perth, Australia, 1932).

17. *Review of Reviews,* Australian edition, March, 1895, 283–87.

18. *Bully Hayes, Buccaneer,* 29.

19. "One day Hayes had a row with the steward (one Jenssen). He was a hot-tempered man. 'By God, I'll shoot you,' says he, and goes down the companion for his revolver. 'Kill him,' said the lady, who had also had a tiff with the hot-tempered fellow. So Jenssen picked up an iron boom crutch, and as Hayes' bald head appeared clove in his skull. And they hove him over the side alive."—*Daily News,* London, August 15, 1896.

20. *Adventure,* New York, September, 1914.

Chapter Seven

1. Sydney *Bulletin,* February 27, 1913, 2.

2. Becke's stories which so far have appeared in anthologies—in addition to those in the Mackaness collection, *Tales from the South Seas* (1929)—include the following: "The Last Cruise of John Maudsley, Recruiter" in *By Creek and Gully* (London, 1899), ed. "Lala Fisher" [Mrs. F. G. Richardson]; "Long Charley's Good Little Wife" in *"Bulletin" Story Book: A Selection of Stories and Literary Sketches from the "Bulletin," 1880–1901* (Sydney, 1901); "Luck" in *Steady and Strong: Stories Told by G. A. Henty and Others* (London, 1905); "A North Pacific Lagoon Island" in *Ile Christmas,* ed. Rev. E. Rougier (London, 1914); "The Chilean Bluejacket" and "The Great Crushing at Mount Sugar-bag" in *Stories of the South Seas,* ed. E. C. Parnwell (London, 1928); "The Fate of the 'Alida'" in *Australian Short Stories,* ed. George Mackaness; "The Rangers of the Tia Kau" in *The Spell of the Pacific,* ed. Carl Stroven and A. Grove Day (New York, 1949); and "At a Kava-Drinking" in *Best South Sea Stories,* ed. A. Grove Day and Carl Stroven (New York, 1964).

3. "The Pit of Maota," in *The Call of the South,* 211.

4. Elsie Noble Caldwell, *Last Witness for Robert Louis Stevenson* (Norman, Oklahoma, 1960), 53.

5. Undated holograph letter from Vailima, in Dixson Letters.

6. *Brown Men and Women* (London, 1898), 2.

7. Unidentified clipping released by Unwin about the time of the publication of Becke's uniform edition in 1924. Probably the letter was written before 1896, because Conrad added that he had a great curiosity to read *A First Fleet Family.*

8. Becke's manuscript is clear even when he is hurriedly writing a letter, and copy for printer is usually impeccable, even a year or two before his death—an important skill in the days before the typewriter. His daughter Niya wrote me on December 31, 1963: "My father's handwriting was extremely clear. He wrote with a folded piece of blotting-paper under each line, and every one was perfectly regular, the letters carefully formed and resembling rows of fish scales."

9. "Confession and Avoidance," *Literary World,* August 13, 1897.

10. Interview in *The Field,* March, 1897.

11. "The Romance of the Outlands," CCIII (July-October, 1905), 67–68.

12. "'Lots o' Time,'" in *'Neath Austral Skies,* 267–71.

13. "'Bay o' Fundy Days,'" in *Notes from My South Sea Log,* 13–14. Becke's service on a New Bedford whaler is otherwise undocumented.

14. Letter in *Adventure*, September, 1914.
15. But as an interviewer commented: "Becke, by the way, is not, as might be expected, *persona non grata* with the missionaries. On the contrary, he is a warm friend, especially of two of the most noted missionaries of the London Missionary Society—the Rev. Frank Lawes of Savage Island, and the Rev. Dr. Turner, once a well-known medical missionary in Samoa."—*Free Lance*, Melbourne, June 18, 1896.
16. *The Tapu of Banderah*, 245–57.
17. *Old Friends, Old Books, Old Sydney* (Sydney, 1952), by James R. Tyrell, 44.
18. *Free Lance*, Melbourne, June 18, 1896.
19. "Harold Frederic: A Tribute," Sydney *Evening News*, November 30, 1898.
20. Introduction to *Moby Dick* (London, 1901).
21. *Bookman* (U.S.), LXII (February, 1926), 674–77.
22. *Quarto Club Papers*, Mount Vernon, New York, III (November, 1930), 100–122.
23. Introduction to *The Spell of the Pacific*, ed. Carl Stroven and A. Grove Day (New York, 1949), ix.
24. *Rascals in Paradise* (New York, 1957), by James A. Michener and A. Grove Day, 213–74; bibliographies, 358–59.
25. *Ishmael* (New York, 1956), 132.
26. "Bully Hayes, Louis Becke, and the Earl of Pembroke," pamphlet, Adelaide, South Australia, 1914.
27. *The Pacific*, ed. Charles Barrett (Melbourne, n.d.), 165–66.
28. Sydney, 1961, 461–64 and *passim*.
29. London, 1961.
30. "Yorke the Adventurer," 97.
31. "An Adventure in the New Hebrides," in *Rídan the Devil*, 215.

Selected Bibliography

PRIMARY SOURCES

Because no complete bibliography of Becke has ever been published, an attempt has been made to be fairly complete here through 1965, at the risk of including fugitive items. Most of the materials in Becke's books previously appeared in Australian, British, or American periodicals. Only the dates of first editions of books are given here, in the above order. In 1924 T. Fisher Unwin in London began issuing a collected, unnumbered edition of Becke's books, starting with *By Reef and Palm* and *The Ebbing of the Tide* in a single volume. All my notes, manuscripts, and microfilms have been deposited in the Gregg M. Sinclair Library of the University of Hawaii and may be examined by qualified persons.

Unpublished

"Large Clipping Book" in Mitchell Library, Sydney, a folio ledger with numbered pages, in which have been pasted clippings of news articles, reviews, stories, "London Notes," etc., undoubtedly kept by Becke, since labels are in his handwriting.

"Small Clipping Book" in Mitchell Library, containing reviews, news items, etc., apparently kept by someone interested in Becke's career.

Other material on Becke in the Mitchell Library includes some letters from him to his mother, other miscellaneous letters, autobiographical notes, agreements with publishers, and half a dozen photographs of the author.

"Typescript," bound 111-page copy of letters, newspaper articles, bibliography, etc., obtained from Mitchell Library in 1937 and now in Gregg M. Sinclair Library, University of Hawaii. Especially of interest are letters to his mother, 1880–1882; "Some Memories" by Becke; letters and contracts concerning the publication of some works; and "Autobiographical Notes in Becke's Own Hand."

"Dixson Letters," in Dixson Library, Sydney, a bundle of letters to Becke from almost a score of correspondents, as well as some manuscripts by Becke and his letter of protest to T. A. Browne ("Rolf Boldrewood") concerning the use of material in Browne's *A Modern Buccaneer.*

"Becke-Jeffery Letters," a collection from the Australian National Library of 351 letters to Walter James Jeffery between October 13, 1895, and March 12, 1901. Two letters apparently belonging with this set, dated June 13, 1899, and January 19, 1900, were kindly supplied by Dr. George Mackaness, who also furnished a letter from Becke to William Dymock, Sydney bookseller, of September 1, 1897, and two letters to Jeffery from A. B. "Banjo" Paterson, Becke's attorney.

"Jamaica Letters," written by Becke to his family in Ireland during July-October, 1902, while on a trip to Jamaica and Canada.

Collections

Mackaness, George (ed.), *Tales from the South Seas by Louis Becke,* with introduction. London: T. Nelson & Sons, 1929. Stories included are: "Bully Hayes," "A Bar of Common Soap," "The Prospector," "The Rangers of the Tia Kau," "Luliban of the Pool," "A Tale of a Mask," "Ninia," "The River of Dreams," "Rodman the Boatsteerer," "An Island Memory," "In a Samoan Village," "The Shadows of the Dead," "For We Were Friends Always," "Nikoa," "Strange White Woman of Maduro," "Arm of Luno Capál," and "Treasure of Don Bruno."

Books

By Reef and Palm. London: T. Fisher Unwin, Autonym Library, 1894. Philadelphia: J. B. Lippincott, 1900. Paris: Dujarrie et Cie., 1908 (*Scenes de la vie Polynesiene,* translated by H. Chateau).

The Ebbing of the Tide: South Sea Stories. London: Unwin, 1895. Philadelphia: Lippincott, 1900.

His Native Wife. Sydney: Alex Lindsay, Australander Library No. 1, 1895. London: Unwin, 1896, Century Library. Philadelphia: Lippincott, 1897.

Pacific Tales. London: Unwin, 1897. New York: New Amsterdam Book Co., 1897. Stockholm: T. & G. Beijers, 1898 (*Hvita Män Och Bruna Kvinnor, Berättelser fran Söderhafsöarne,* translated by Hans Cavallin).

Wild Life in Southern Seas. London: Unwin, 1897. New York: New Amsterdam Book Co., 1898.

Rodman the Boatsteerer and Other Stories. London: Unwin, 1898. Philadelphia: Lippincott, 1924.

Derricourt, William. *Old Convict Days.* London: Unwin, 1899. Foreword and conclusion by Louis Becke.

Rídan the Devil and Other Stories. London: Unwin, 1899.

Tom Wallis, a Tale of the South Seas. London: Religious Tract Society [1900].

Edward Barry, South Sea Pearler. London: Unwin, 1900. Boston: L. C. Page and Co., 1900.

Melville, Herman. *Moby Dick.* London: G. P. Putnam's Sons, 1901. Introduction by Louis Becke.

Tessa [and] *The Trader's Wife.* London: Unwin, 1901.

By Rock and Pool on an Austral Shore. London: Unwin, 1901.

Yorke the Adventurer, and Other Stories. London: Unwin, 1901. Philadelphia: Lippincott, 1925.

Breachley, Black Sheep. London: Unwin, 1902.

The Strange Adventure of James Shervinton, and Other Stories. London: Unwin, 1902. Philadelphia: Lippincott, 1926.

The "Jalasco" Brig. London: Anthony Traherne, 1902.

Helen Adair. London: Unwin, 1903. Philadelphia: Lippincott, 1903.

Chinkie's Flat and Other Stories. London: Unwin, 1904.

Tom Gerrard. London: Unwin, 1904.

Under Tropic Skies. London: Unwin [1904]. Philadelphia: Lippincott, 1905.

Notes from My South Sea Log. London: T. Werner Laurie, 1905. Philadelphia: Lippincott, 1926.

The Adventures of a Supercargo. London: Unwin, 1906. Philadelphia: Lippincott, 1906.

Sketches from Normandy. London: Laurie, 1906. Philadelphia: Lippincott, 1907.

The Settlers of Karossa Creek, and Other Stories of Australian Bush Life. London: Religious Tract Society [1907].

The Call of the South. London: John Milne, 1908. Philadelphia: Lippincott, 1908.

The Pearl Divers of Roncador Reef. London: James Clarke & Co., 1908.

The Adventures of Louis Blake. London: Laurie, 1909. Philadelphia: Lippincott, 1926.

'Neath Austral Skies. London: Milne, 1909.

Bully Hayes: Buccaneer, and Other Stories. Sydney: New South Wales Bookstall Co., Ltd., 1913; illustrated by Norman Lindsay.

Collaborations With Walter James Jeffery

A First Fleet Family: A Hitherto Unpublished Narrative of Certain Remarkable Adventures Compiled from the Papers of Sergeant William Dew of the Marines, with map and preface. London: Unwin, 1896. New York: Macmillan, 1896.

The Mystery of the Laughlin Islands. London: Unwin, 1896.

The Mutineer: A Romance of Pitcairn Island. London: Unwin, 1898.

The Naval Pioneers of Australia. London: John Murray, 1899.

Admiral Phillip: The Founding of New South Wales. London: Unwin, 1899. Builders of Greater Britain, No. 6. New York: Longmans, 1899.

The Tapu of Banderah. London: C. Arthur Pearson, 1901. Philadelphia: Lippincott, 1901.

SECONDARY SOURCES

Australian Encyclopedia. Sydney: Angus & Robertson, 1958, I, 470–471. Standard biography, probably written by Alec H. Chisholm.

Baird, James R. *Ishmael*. Baltimore: Johns Hopkins Press, 1956. Probably the most important book on primitivism in Pacific literature; Baird considers study of Becke indispensable for an historical approach.

Browne, Thomas A. ["Rolf Boldrewood"] *A Modern Buccaneer*. London: Macmillan, 1894. Much of this novel was based on material written by Becke.

"By Reef and Palm: The Lure of the South Seas in Literature," *John o' London's Weekly*, April 5, 1924. Discusses Becke along with Melville, Loti, Stevenson, and London.

Christian, F. W., "Reminiscences of Louis Becke," *Life*, New Zealand, January, 1927, 8–10, adds little to previously known facts.

Day, A. Grove. "By Reef and Tide: Louis Becke's Critical Reputation," *Australian Letters*, Adelaide, VI (October, 1963), 16–26, shows changes in appreciation and stresses American affiliations of Becke.

Dictionary of Australian Biography, ed. Percival Serle. Sydney: Angus & Robertson, 1947, I, 65–66. Contains some errors deriving from Becke's interviews and autobiographical reports.

Fitzgerald, J. D. *Studies in Australian Crime*, 1st series. Sydney: Angus & Robertson, 1924, 115. Refers to Becke's arrest, "charged with being an accomplice of Bully Hayes in various piracies in the Pacific."

"Funeral of Louis Becke," Sydney *Sun*, February 19, 1913. Main surviving account of funeral ceremony.

Gallagher, Philip. "Lost Years of a Vagabond," Sydney *Morning Herald*,

February 15, 1953, is one of the best brief biographies, based on careful study.

Green, Henry Mackenzie. *A History of Australian Literature,* 2 vol. Sydney: Angus & Robertson, 1961. This recent, authoritative study devotes five pages to Becke and is on the whole highly laudatory.

Hall, James Norman. *My Island Home.* Boston: Little, Brown, 1952. The genesis of the *Bounty* trilogy is here revealed better than anywhere else, and the author states that Nordhoff and Hall were unacquainted with any adult novels about the *Bounty* mutiny.

[Hayes, W. T.] For a bibliography on "Bully" Hayes, see Michener and Day, below.

Heney, T. W. "Tragedy and Comedy: Australian Writers Under Review," Daily *Telegraph,* Sydney, September 8, 1923. The writer, who knew Becke in Sydney and London, concludes that he "really helped to found a school of literature—the Island School."

Ingamells, Rex. "Novelists of the Pacific," in *The Pacific,* ed. Charles Barrett. Melbourne: N. H. Seward [1950?], 157–66. Gives Becke high praise, favoring him over Stevenson because of his "sound knowledge of the islands."

Ingram, Margaret Anne. "Louis Becke, a Study," unpublished Master of Arts Thesis, No. 159, University of Hawaii, Honolulu, 1937. A pioneer general survey under the supervision of Dr. Carl Stroven.

Interview, *Free Lance,* Melbourne, June 6, 1896, signed "Yelwarc." Useful information given just before Becke left for London.

Interview, South Australian *Register,* Adelaide, June 23, 1896. Lengthy and informative account of Becke's adventures in the Pacific.

Interview, London *Daily News,* August 15, 1896. Lengthy account of impression made by Becke when first arriving in London.

Interview, *Daily Gleaner,* Jamaica, B.W.I., August 6, 1902. Mention of Becke's plans for trip and description of personality.

Interview, *Dominion,* Wellington, N.Z., September 9, 1908. Gives account of plans for ethnological expedition to South Pacific.

Interview, *Fiji Times,* Suva, October 4, 1908. Mentions further research plans and interests of Mr. and Mrs. Becke.

"J.C." "Australasian Literature," *Nation,* XCVII (July 10, 1913), 30–31. Fairly useful account sent from Sydney soon after Becke's death there, mentioning types of stories for which he was best known.

Johns, Fred. *An Australian Biographical Dictionary.* Melbourne: Macmillan & Co., 1934, 23. Facts not always reliable.

"The Late Louis Becke, the Dumas of the Pacific," unidentified clipping, Mitchell Library, CLVIII, Pacific Islands, p. 7. Brief account of some value to the biographer.

"Louis Becke." *Pacific Islands Monthly*, II (May, 1932), 10. Contains some bibliographic notes on early editions of Becke's books, reprinted from *Today*.

Lindsay, Norman. "Louis Becke," *Bulletin*, Sydney, September 7, 1955, 2. Reminiscences by famed novelist, who illustrated Becke's *Bully Hayes: Buccaneer*.

Lubbock, Basil. *Bully Hayes*. London: M. Hopkinson, 1931. Fictionized account of the life of the buccaneer, which perpetuates many legends about both Hayes and Becke.

Michener, James A. and A. Grove Day. *Rascals in Paradise*. New York: Random House, 1957. Chapter 7, "Bully Hayes, South Sea Buccaneer," and Chapter 8, "Louis Becke, Adventurer and Writer," are biographies in popular style but based on facts; include bibliographies.

Miller, E. Morris. *Australian Literature*, 2 vol. Melbourne: Melbourne University Press and Oxford Press, 1940. Pioneer work containing excellent bibliographies to that date and many references and critical remarks on Becke, especially pp. 461–64.

———. *Australian Literature: A Bibliography to 1938*, extended to 1950 by Frederick T. Macartney. Sydney: Angus & Robertson, 1956. Becke is mentioned pages 56–58.

"A New Australian Writer, Mr. Louis Becke," *Review of Reviews* (Australian edition), March, 1895, 283–87. A valuable interview before Becke departed for London, contributing much on his life in the Islands and in Australia.

Niau, Josephine H. *The Phantom Paradise*. Sydney: Angus & Robertson, 1936. Best account of ill-fated New Ireland colonization scheme in which Becke stated he had participated.

Obituary, *Argus*, Melbourne, February 20, 1913.

Obituary, *Bookfellow*, Sydney, March 1, 1913.

Obituary, *Bulletin*, Sydney, February 20, 1913, 2. Terse but friendly account, probably written by a former colleague on the *Bulletin*, where Becke's stories first appeared.

Obituary, *Dominion Evening Post*, Wellington, N.Z. February 19, 1913.

Obituary, *Free Lance*, Melbourne, February 22, 1913.

Obituary, Sydney *Morning Herald*, February 19, 1913. Standard newspaper account.

Obituary, Sydney *Daily Telegraph*, February 19, 1913. Fairly accurate; states that South Sea expedition in later years was abandoned "owing to some disagreement with another member of the party."

Obituary, loose clipping, unidentified Port Macquarie newspaper, states Becke had planned to return to his birthplace soon, and cites his daughter Nora as "a very distinguished linguist."

O'Leary, Con. "By Reef and Palm: From Island Trader to Novelist of the Pacific," *T.P.'s & Cassell's Weekly*, London, March 14, 1925. Review of Becke's life and work on the occasion of Unwin's issue of a collected edition.

Pembroke, Earl of (George Robert Charles Herbert). Introduction to first edition of *By Reef and Palm*. Based on notes furnished by Becke, lacking dates and often highly unreliable in biographical details.

Pottle, Frederick A. *Boswell and the Girl from Botany Bay*. New York: Viking, 1937.

Priday, Lew. "Trader Becke of the South Seas," *Bulletin*, Sydney, June 15, 1955, 25. Good account by a former Island trader, and cites letter of October 1, 1892, in which Becke applied for post in New Hebrides.

Reeves, Edward. *Brown Men and Women, or the South Sea Islands in 1895 and 1896*. London: S. Sonnenschein & Co., 1898. Pays tribute to Becke in Chapter 1 as the author "who knew the Pacific as few men alive or dead have ever known it!"

Riesenfeld, Victor. "Louis Becke," *Quarto Club Papers*, Mount Vernon, New York, III (November, 1930), 100–122. Account honeycombed with errors revealing dangers of using Becke's work as autobiography, but the spirit is one of marked admiration. Bibliography is mere listing of a few books.

Rinehart, Alan. "Legend of Adventure," *Bookman*, New York, LXII (February, 1926), 674–77. An appreciation by an American who felt Becke had been forgotten and should be read.

Roderick, Colin. *Introduction to Australian Fiction*. Sydney: Angus & Robertson, 1951, 45–47. Good general account, but limits value of Becke's writing to early short stories and to *A First Fleet Family*.

Saunders, A. T. "Bully Hayes, Louis Becke, and the Earl of Pembroke," pamphlet, Adelaide, South Australia, 1914. Vigorous attempt, based on documents but still not always correct in conclusions, to show growth of legends; places much reliance on Earl of Pembroke's introduction to *By Reef and Palm* (see above).

Stephens, A. G. Article in *Bookfellow*, Sydney, April, 1920, 89. Severely censures T. A. Browne for not acknowledging the contribution of Becke to *A Modern Buccaneer*.

[Stewart, Douglas]. Reprint of review of *By Reef and Palm* in Sydney *Bulletin*, Sydney, August 17, 1955, 2. Useful criticism of Becke's work by one of Australia's foremost poets, playwrights, and reviewers.

Stone, Walter W. "Becke's Letter to Boldrewood." *Biblionews*, Sydney,

V (March, 1952). Stone states that Lindsay (see above) had confused Becke's death with that of another writer, and that Becke died of cancer of the throat.

Trapp, Phyllis Burney. "Some Account of the Writings of Louis Becke: being a thesis presented for the Jacob Joseph Scholarship, 1931." Wellington, New Zealand, 1931. A student production of little original contribution but some careful reading.

Tyrrell, James. *Old Books, Old Friends, Old Sydney*. Sydney: Angus & Robertson, 1952. Brief mention of Becke, whom Tyrrell met in Sydney and London.

Wright, Edward. "The Romance of the Outlands," *Quarterly Review*, London, CCIII (July-October, 1905), 67–68. Article dealing with writers of period who described "outposts of empire" mentions Becke at some length.

Index

(Fictitious persons, places, or ships are not indexed.)